I0474114

Stewardship Economy   2

valuing land and
managing transition

Julian Pratt

Published by

Editorial note

This book brings together previously unpublished material which
Julian worked on alongside the summary book, *Stewardship
Economy 1: private property without private ownership*. With
the other five books in the series, it provides the additional
material that lies behind the proposals and assertions made in
book 1. Unfortunately, aspects of this work are unfinished, some
of the examples provided are out of date, there is some repetition
of text and some references (bibliography in book 7) are not
available. I hope you, the reader, will excuse this and will find
the work as a whole thought-provoking and topical.

Rosemary Field

September 2021

ISBN 978-1-4717-0265-5

Contents

Stewardship Economy

The Stewardship Economy series of books questions one of the foundations on which market-based economies rest: the system of property rights. It suggests that the form of private property that works well for the things that we make is both unethical and inefficient when we apply it to land and the rest of the natural world. It proposes an alternative to ownership – stewardship.

The underlying principle of stewardship is that everyone is entitled to an equal share of the wealth of the natural world. The steward of any part of the natural world has the secure and exclusive right to use it, the responsibility to care for it and the duty to compensate others for excluding them from it.

In practical terms this means that stewards of land pay fees that are equal to its market rent. These fees provide revenue that may be used to provide government with an income that is an alternative to orthodox taxation and, ideally, to provide everyone with a (small) Universal Income. Stewards of environmental resources pay fees equal to their resource rent, and this revenue is distributed to everyone as an Environmental Dividend.

Books in the series

Stewardship Economy 1: private property without private ownership is the first book and provides an overall summary of the main ideas.

Stewardship Economy 2: Valuing land and managing transition (this book) sets out in some detail how to establish the market rent of land and how to make the transition from an ownership to a stewardship economy. It also considers how the revenue from stewardship fees might be distributed.

Stewardship Economy 3: Land, environment and climate explores how a stewardship economy would transform the way we use land, provide housing and develop our cities. It goes on to consider how stewardship would help address pressing environmental and climate concerns.

Stewardship Economy 4: The economy, wealth and universal income focuses on the impact of stewardship on the national and global economy, how the distribution of wealth would be changed and the impact of a Universal Income.

Stewardship Economy 5: efficient, fair taxes and the role of the state describes the some of the adverse effects of our current system of taxation and considers the role of the state in a stewardship economy.

Stewardship Economy 6: property rights describes the systems of property rights in our current economic system, their history and how property rights could be more fair and efficient in a stewardship economy.

Stewardship Economy 7: some economics explained, economic terms and bibliography. This book provides an introduction to some key economic concepts for the non-specialist and lists the references, as far as they are available.

Introduction

The idea of 'ownership' works well enough for the things we make. *Stewardship Economy 1: Private Property without Private Ownership* and other books in the series challenge the assumption that it is appropriate to apply the same concept of ownership to the natural world (land and the environment).

This book proposes an alternative, 'stewardship'. The underlying principle of stewardship is that everyone is entitled to an equal share of the wealth of the natural world. In a stewardship economy, things made by people, for example tables and houses, are held in the form of private property with which we are familiar – ownership. The natural world, including the land, oceans, rivers and atmosphere, is held in stewardship.

The steward of any part of the natural world has:

- the right to occupy and use it

- the responsibility to care for it

- the duty to pay stewardship fees, equal to the market rent, for its use (which compensates others for excluding them from it)

- ownership, in the conventional sense, of any buildings or other improvements.

In practical terms this means that the land is held in trust and stewards of land pay fees. The revenue from these fees replaces most other taxes to fund government expenditure and any surplus is distributed to everyone as a Universal Income. The environment is also held in trust and anyone who uses it pays fees that are equal to the market rent of that resource. The revenue that is generated is distributed to everyone as an Environmental Dividend or invested for future generations.

In situations where land is not owned or where ownership is not strongly contested, setting up and maintaining a stewardship economy would not be a difficult or challenging. But introducing stewardship into an ownership economy will require the unravelling of a complex tax-benefit system and overcoming the political resistance mounted by those who are favoured by this economy. It will inevitably be a complex and difficult challenge. Transition from ownership to stewardship could follow several very different paths, and each of these needs to be described in detail and their consequences modelled. Above all, it will be necessary for transition to take place very gradually (likely over 25 years or more) to minimise the impact felt by landowners who would, over time, see the value of their land fall to zero.

One reason that people may be drawn to the principles of a stewardship economy is that they have a passion for social justice and the desire to do something about poverty and inequalities. They recognise that stewardship would stimulate the economy by removing dysfunctional taxes and making land available to those who want to use it. They see that it would protect the environment by putting a price on environmental goods and so influence economic decision-making. And they support the sharing of the product of the global economy among all people by replacing conditional benefit systems with a Universal Income.

Another reason that people come to stewardship is the result of asking a different question, something like 'how can people live in harmony as part of an earth community (Jonty Williams 2014:26)?' This must be a question which resonates particularly with the current focus on sustaining our environment and the need to address climate change. In addition to the importance of paying fees for the use of land, Jonty Williams proposes that the tenure of all land should be subject to husbandry clauses that specify the steward's duties to care for the land (2014:24).

The book describes how land is valued at present and how this could be achieved in a stewardship economy, including valuation for tradable emissions permits. It explore show the transition to a stewardship economy may be achieved and outlines how the revenue might be spent.

I draw on lessons from property taxation in ownership economies, which are explored in Part I (Chapters 1 & 2). There are well established valuation methods, described in Part II (Chapters 3 & 4), that provide entirely practical ways to tax up to perhaps 50 per cent of the market rent of land. Chapter 5 describes attempts to estimate the market rent of the whole of the UK.

Part III (Chapters 6-9) looks at how valuation could operate in a stewardship economy. Collecting 100 per cent of the market rent, as advocated in *Stewardship Economy* and other books in the series, is a much more radical proposal than collecting 50 per cent, both politically and practically. It requires new arrangements for land transfers that are integrated with the valuation process – a New Land Market.

If 100 per cent of the market rent of land is collected as fees then the market value (sale price) of that land is zero (Chapter 6). Critics correctly point out that this would destroy the land market as we know it. They also suggest, incorrectly, that this makes it impossible in a stewardship economy for prices to be established that would allocate land efficiently. This book describes a new sort of land market that avoids these problems by determining both market rent and the allocation of land in a single market transaction. This New Land Market makes it possible to collect 100 per cent of the market rent without eroding the tax base or compromising the efficient use of land.

Part IV (Chapter 10) takes climate change as an example of environmental stewardship. It discusses how tradable emissions permits could be used to limit climate change in a stewardship economy and contrasts this approach with the existing European Emissions Trading Scheme.

The final Part V (Chapters 11-15) discusses some of the challenges and options for making the transition from ownership to stewardship. It concludes that it would be technically possible to arrange transition in a way that ensures owners retain the full current value of their properties but forgo any future increases, which would be used to provide government revenue and a small Universal Income.

The principle of stewardship applies to environmental resources just as to land. The current move, in ownership economies, from the gifting (grandfathering) of emissions permits to auctioning is the right approach to the allocation of access to the environment (Chapter 14). To avoid the impression that this is a stealth tax (Chapter 10), the revenue from permits to use renewable resources should not be used to provide additional income for government but should be distributed on an equal per capita basis as an Environmental Dividend.

The full bibliography is in book 7.

Part I   Lessons from ownership

Ownership economies provide many examples of how *not* to capture the value of land for the common good, as well as some positive examples. Part I of this book draws on these examples to identify lessons for capturing the value of land in a Stewardship Economy.

Chapter 1 sets out the conditions that are necessary to collect stewardship fees, or indeed any tax on land. Chapter 2 explores the variety of approaches taken to the capture of land value. Chapter 3 explains how the market rent of the UK can be estimated.

Chapter 1 Necessary conditions for collection of stewardship fees

For any sort of tax or charge on the market rent of land to be possible, whether this is only part of the value or full stewardship fees, some necessary conditions need to be in place:

- a system of enforceable property rights

- a register of who has legal title to each site, its value and any planning constraints

- a mechanism for transferring title (Chapter 9).

Enforceable property rights

When people buy and sell land it is a bundle of property rights referred to as 'legal title' that is being transferred. In an ownership economy this is encapsulated in the liberal conception of private ownership.

In low-consumption economies title is often customary rather than legally recognised and enforceable. Some 80 per cent of the countryside in low-consumption economies may have no legally recognised owner. Two thirds of the residents of Mexico City have no proper title deeds (Economist 1995: 70);   and in Tanzania titling systems overlap and contradict each other.

A satisfactory titling system, particularly one that is open to interrogation by the public, is a valuable resource in its own right – particularly in low- consumption economies. Secure legal title provides incentives for owners to improve their property and makes it possible for a land market to operate, as well as being a necessary step towards borrowing against the value of the property or raising charges or taxes on the value of land.

In high-consumption economies most land has an identifiable owner and property rights are enforceable in law.

A register of the ownership and value of land

The registration of title to land has a long history that goes back to tomb inscriptions in Egypt from around 3000 BCE.

This section outlines the history and current state of information about land ownership and highlights the need for a publicly accessible comprehensive database.

Historical

Roman

The Romans' most important system for raising revenue, tributum soli, was a land tax imposed on their provinces. They established registers of land ownership, and registration was most fully developed in Roman Egypt where it extended to include the registration of conveyances and mortgages. The Romans registered land and collected tribute in both England and Wales, but the practice ceased after the Roman withdrawal.

Anglo-Saxon

During the Anglo-Saxon period a tax on land again provided the main source of revenue. In 991, after his defeat at the Battle of Maldon, Æthelred the Unready was forced to pay tribute to the Danes, later known as Danegeld. In 1012 he introduced a tax to support the army, Heregeld. The geld was financed by a tax on each hide, the amount of land that was needed to support one family, and which was therefore a Land Value Tax. This required a record of land ownership to be maintained throughout most of the Angle-Saxon period, though the payment of tribute was intermittent.

Domesday

After the Norman Conquest a similar tax based on the value of land was re-introduced and remained the main form of taxation until 1162 when it was replaced by taxes on income and moveable property. William ordered the great survey of 1086, summarised in the two books that came to be called Domesday. This was much more than the geld book that would be required to levy a tax on land, as it documented feudal rights and established legal title to land. But one of the purposes of the survey was to itemise the resources and taxable values of the manors and boroughs, including information about livestock, the names of sub-tenants and numbers of serfs. It covered a small part of Wales and most of England apart from London, Winchester, Durham and Northumberland.

Land Registration

Although Domesday continues to be admissible in law and has been called in evidence in the 20th century, most claims to property rights in England and Wales from the 11th to the 20th centuries were established by means of title deeds. The Statute of Enrolments (1535) required enrolment of deeds with the keeper for the rolls for the country, though this was widely avoided. In the 17th century there were many calls for county registries, and several were established (Mayer & Pemberton 2000:6).

In Scotland registers had been kept in Edinburgh Castle from the 13th century and a national public register of deeds, the Register of Sasines, was established in 1617. Land registration in Scotland is now handled by Registers of Scotland.

A Royal Commission on the Registration of Title in 1857 proposed setting up a registry for England and Wales to provide proof of ownership of particular plots of land in case of dispute, and to facilitate conveyancing. A series of Land Registration Acts from 1862 to 2002 established and modified the remit of the Land Registry.

Registration in England and Wales was initially voluntary and proceeded very slowly, until the Land Transfer Act (1897) made it compulsory (with a county veto). Compulsory registration in London was introduced in 1899 and gradually extended to include the whole of England and Wales by 1990. Compulsory registration does not mean that all land has to be registered but that registration has to take place when certain triggers occur, most importantly when ownership is transferred. A variety of interests in land may be registered; most importantly freehold, mortgages and leaseholds of more than seven years.

One of the reasons that registration has taken so long is that the Land Registry is required by government to be self-financing, receiving most of its income from fees levied at the time when ownership of land is transferred, leaving it underfunded for a role that would be central to the economy if the importance of land as a factor in the economy was widely recognised.

Unlike Domesday the registry was not originally intended to provide a comprehensive overview of land ownership, but it is now not far from doing just that. The Land Registry has the resources to complete the registration of all land within a couple of years if it had the mandate to do so (Payne, R. 2012).

The 1872 return

A remarkably successful attempt to take stock of the ownership of more or less the whole country (not including unrated land or London) was made in the 1872 Return of Owners of Land (HMSO 1873-1876).

Its origins lie in the 1861 census. Only thirty thousand people described themselves as landowners (Kevin Cahill 2002/3: 30), and this led the Anti Corn Law campaigner John Bright to claim that the country was owned by a very small proportion of the population. To refute this argument the 15th Earl of Derby proposed that the government take steps to ascertain the number of proprietors of land and houses and the extent of their property holdings.

The information was already held at parish level in valuation lists and rate books, but the compilers of the Return recognised that there were defects due to errors, omissions and duplications in the original lists (Kevin Cahill 2002/3: 34).

The first edition of John Bateman's Great Landowners of Great Britain and Ireland (John Bateman 1873), drawing on Return of Owners of Land, consolidated and corrected the landholdings of those owning more than 3000 acres, who numbered only about 1500. He also calculated that, including peers, great landowners, squires, yeomen and small proprietors there were about 250,000 landowners; nearly a million if cottagers with less than an acre were included (Kevin Cahill 2002/3: 45).

The Return proved threatening to landowners by confirming the degree of concentration of land ownership and was successfully criticised for its flaws. It nevertheless remains the most thorough and extensive record of landholdings in the UK and Ireland ever to be produced. Kenneth Cahill points out that in 1876 there was universal free access to the names and addresses of the owners of 95 per cent of the land area of the United Kingdom of Great Britain and Ireland in local parish offices and libraries (Kevin Cahill 2002/3: 29). Far less information is publicly available today, though both Kevin Cahill (UK) and Andy Wightman (Scotland) (Andy Wightman 2011) provide a wealth of information.

Contemporary

Tony Vickers (2009:74) summarised the state and availability (or otherwise) of information about land ownership and land value in Britain that would be required for a tax on land values (a fiscal cadastre). His summary of the relevant datasets (next page) indicates the task that would be required in bringing them all together:

Dataset	British name	Provider agency (Eng &Wales)	Government Department
Mapping	MasterMapTM	Ordnance Survey	Communities & Local Government
Addressing	National Land and Property Gazetteer	Local government	Communities & Local Government
Ownership	Land Registers	Land Registry	Justice
Valuation	Tax lists	Valuation Office Agency (VOA)	H M Treasury
Current use	National Land Use Database (NLUD)	Not available	Communities & Local Government
Planning (permissions & restrictions)	Not available	Local government	Communities & Local Government

Mapping

Ordnance Survey completed digital mapping of Britain in 1995 and by 2001 developed the first national large-scale structured geographical data set in the world, MasterMapTM. Containing half a million polygons, surveys are electronic, and it is continuously updated (Tony Vickers 2009: 74).

A key question for governments is how to treat the intellectual property rights held by the public sector, such as the copyright held by Ordnance Survey. It may be treated as an asset to be made available freely or at marginal cost, which maximises its use and subsidises its users. Or it may be treated as a commodity that enables its owner to become self-financing or profit-making. There are arguments each way, but the European Union has resolved to follow the marginal cost route; and in the USA the more generous availability of data than in the UK appears to result in greater economic activity, with an increase in tax revenues that exceeds any loss of direct revenue. The commodification of the Ordnance Survey's intellectual property appears to have been the cause of a 20 year friction between the elements of the British geographical information industry (Tony Vickers 2009:78) that was resolved with the removal of charges in 2010.

Addressing

The National Land and Property Gazetteer claims that it provides the first comprehensive address base for all commercial and residential buildings in Great Britain to have been compiled since 1086. It is an authoritative national address list that provides unique identification of land and property. It is the central hub for the Local Land and Property Gazetteers which are held by the address-creating local authorities.

It provides a list of Basic Land and Property Units (BLPUs), areas of land in uniform property rights (which may be implied if the property rights are unclear) and assigns each a Unique Property Reference Number (UPRN). These may refer to non-postally-addressed objects such as parks, churches, public buildings and war memorials as well as to buildings.

Ownership

The National Land Information Service was initially intended to bring together many sources of information about land, but ultimately the only function that has been implemented is that of providing online searches for the purposes of conveyancing.

Well over 95 per cent of households in England and Wales now live in properties registered with the Land Registry but substantial amounts of rural land, owned by a relatively small number of large and institutional landowners including the state, remains unregistered. In 2001 about half the area of England and Wales, amounting to about 2 million titles (Kevin Cahill 2002/3: 53), was not registered. Since then, there has been considerable progress with voluntary registration, and by 2017 more than 85 per cent of the land mass of England and Wales had been registered.

Most of the addressing and ownership information is now available, but it is held in different places. It could be brought together, given the political will.

Valuation

Information about the price at which properties (buildings + land) are transferred is not readily available to the public. It is held in many places, for example, estate agents and back copies of advertisements in newspapers, but the main source is now the internet.

The Valuation Office Agency, an agency of the HM Revenue and Customs, is responsible for valuations for National Non-Domestic (Business) Rates, Council Tax, Inheritance Tax and Capital Gains Tax. It produces twice-yearly Property Market Reports that provide valuations of typical properties across the UK but does not provide separate valuations for land and buildings.

Local Authorities hold valuation registers for residential, commercial and business land that enable them to levy the Council Tax and the Non-Domestic (Business) Rate.

The Land Registry was not opened to the public till 1990. It holds information about the price for which registered properties were last sold (the Price Paid Dataset). This may not, however, represent an open market transaction, does not separate land from buildings and is difficult to convert into a current value.

This dataset forms the basis for the Land Registry's UK House Price Index, but public access to information at any level of detail other than individual sites and national aggregates remains prohibitively expensive. In addition, the Land Registry has entered into commercial arrangements with private sector providers, giving them access to its bulk data which allow them to provide additional services such as updated valuations and the values of comparables using an Automated Value Model (www.mouseprice.com).

A stewardship economy requires that the value of both the improvements and the market rent of the land should be assessed, and recorded, separately. This information is not available in the UK, though it has been produced in other jurisdictions where Land Value Taxation has been introduced into an ownership economy (Chapter 2).

In spite of the aspirations for the National Land Use Database (NLUD), there are no consolidated data available about current land use.

It would be easier to record present and permitted uses if it were possible to adopt a standardised land use classification. But this is more difficult in the UK than in countries like the USA, where zoning restrictions are much broader in scope and less specific to individual properties.

Planning (permitted use)

The core of the planning system are the Local Planning Authorities – mainly county, borough and unitary authorities – which produce Local Plans and have a statutory duty to co-operate. On a regional or national scale, the only guidance is provided by the National Planning Policy Framework, which is not prescriptive but is deemed to be a 'material consideration' that Local Planning Authorities must take in to account. At a national level the Planning Inspectorate on behalf of the Secretary of State for Communities and Local Government is responsible for significant infrastructure projects and for hearing appeals from the Local Planning Authorities.

The Localism Act 2011 introduced the option of Neighbourhood Plans that are more local than Local Plans.

Information about planning restrictions and consents for an individual site may be held by the planning department of the Local Authority. There may be additional restrictions in the form of restrictive covenants included in the title deeds, which may be noted in the current entry in the Land Register.

Geographic Information Systems

A Geographic Information System (GIS) is a system for capturing, storing, checking, manipulating, analysing and displaying data that are spatially referenced to the Earth. It usually takes the form of a database linked with digitised map data and a high-resolution graphics output.

A Geographic Information System has many possible uses. It can be used for thematic mapping – for example flood risk, pollution levels or disease-specific mortality rates can be stored in the database and displayed geographically, providing early warning of environmental or health problems. The most pressing use will probably be in predicting the economic impact of climate change and planning how to adapt to it. The possibilities are limited only by the implications for civil liberties.

Geographic Information Systems are used by land titles offices, such as the Land Registry, who use a Unique Property Reference Number (UPRN) to link the geographic display with its database entry. The geographic display may be quite sophisticated - for example it may present a map of a country and the user may then zoom down to whatever resolution they wish, right down to an individual housing plot. Alternatively, plots of land may be identified through the database, for example by address or owner.

A Geographic Information System, covering the whole country and administered locally, has clear benefits for a variety of purposes including public health, flood risk analysis and a wide range of commercial applications as well as recording valuations for the purposes of stewardship.

A stewardship economy requires a database of land ownership and values that is freely available to anyone who wants to consult it, including people interested in buying or selling properties and researchers. It would include, for each property:

- Unique Property Reference Number (UPRN)
- location (grid co-ordinates)
- unique address
- dimensions
- boundaries
- present use
- permitted uses
- value of land
- value of buildings and other improvements
- owner
- leasehold interests.

The need for an integrated database of this sort is not contentious. The European Union's Inspire Directive (2007) aims to develop European Union-wide information to enable sharing of spatial information, particularly for the purpose of developing environmental policy. The government's location strategy (Communities and Local Government 2008) goes further, identifying land registration and property valuation amongst the key data sets that need to be able to be shared.

Distributed databases – Blockchain technology

Land Registries are databases that have been held on paper and digitally. The World Bank estimates that 70 per cent of the world's population has no access to secure land titling, and in some countries central databases have been hacked, often by officials who have benefited from corrupt land transfers –

particularly those involving desirable housing plots and areas rich in natural resources.

Blockchain technology, such as that underpinning Bitcoin, offers the opportunity of creating a theoretically incorruptible database that is stored on multiple computers. It has the additional advantage that transactions in the database can be initiated by those involved, allowing the bottom-up creation of a Land Registry that may include informal claims. Several countries have taken the development of a blockchain-based national Land Registry into a pilot phase including Honduras, Georgia and Sweden.

Implications for a stewardship economy

Secure legal title and a comprehensive publicly accessible database of land ownership are essential requirements for any charge or tax on land. Both legal titles and a database are needed in an ownership economy if there is to be efficient handling of the ownership and transfer of land, so these systems should not represent additional costs of stewardship.

Given the political intent at European and national level to produce a comprehensive database of land, and the existing datasets, it should be possible to develop a Geographic Information System capable of hosting valuations for stewardship.

Chapter 2 Land Value Capture

The purpose of this chapter is to set stewardship fees in the wider context of the variety of ways in which the state has captured the value of land and its uplift. The chapter explores what we mean by land value capture, who is able to benefit and in what circumstances. It explains why market rent is preferable to market value as a measure of the value of land and considers briefly several examples of how land value has been captured. Using this background, it then explores the lessons for capturing land value in a stewardship economy.

Property taxes of one sort or another provided most of the revenue that was used to fund both the state and religious institutions from the onset of settled agriculture until the introduction of income taxes at the end of the 18th century. Since that time there have been many attempts to raise revenue from land and the environment. One approach is for the state or other public body to own the land in question. Another is a one-off fee or charge when the state intervenes in a way that causes an uplift in land value, for example by granting planning permission or providing infrastructure. These fees are relatively easy to justify and implement but impose transaction costs, provide opportunities for corruption and are inefficient.

A third approach is to impose some form of property tax, paid on a regular basis and based on the value of the whole property (land plus buildings). Most property taxes that have been implemented, including the current Council Tax and National Non-Domestic (Business) Rates, are strikingly different from a Land Value Tax or stewardship fees because the valuation is based on current use, there are many exemptions and reliefs, and they include a tax on buildings.

These taxes provide lessons for the design and implementation of stewardship fees, and this chapter draws out these lessons.

What do we mean by Land Value Capture?

Land value capture enables communities to recover and reinvest land value increases that result from public investment and government actions. https://www.oecd.org/cfe/cities/Flyer-Land-Value-Capture.pdf

If the value of land, as opposed to secure tenure of that land, is the absolute property of its owner then the community has no claim over any of its value if this increases for any reason. If secure tenure is qualified by some duties to the community, these duties may include the requirement to share some of the uplift in value that occurs from time to time.

There is disagreement about land ownership and development rights between two groups in most high-consumption economies. One group sees private ownership as absolute (and perpetual). This group tends to be made up of landowners, potential landowners, developers, the professional interests that support them and politicians of the right. The other group understands the importance of security of tenure to private property but regards the value of the land as something that is created by, and is the rightful property of, that community. They tend to be the landless, groups campaigning on their behalf, local authorities with the responsibility for providing services (particularly housing) for their communities and politicians of the left.

Owners

he fundamental ethical argument, accepted at present by most people, is that ownership of land is no different from ownership of the things that we make, artefacts. If an artefact, say a painting or a piece of furniture, increases in value no one disputes that the increase in its value belongs to its owner. Surely the same applies to a plot of land?

This argument is reinforced by the 'right to property' enshrined in the French Declaration of the Rights of Man and of the Citizen (1789) and the UN Universal Declaration of Human Rights (1948). If the 'right to property' means the right to retain, perpetually and unconditionally, any property that has been legally acquired then it must surely be wrong for the community or the state to claim any of the value of that property, whether artefacts or natural property.

Planning law varies from country to country, and in the UK seems to favour a limited claim to development rights by the owner (below). Human rights law may trump planning law even though the 'human right' described in the French constitution was the general right not to be excluded from the class of property-owners, for example on the grounds of being a woman, rather than the special right to a particular property as the result of having fulfilled a specific action such as being the first occupant.

Community

Many people recognise that, at least under certain specific circumstances, the community has an ethical claim on an uplift in land value. One of these is where the state is considering providing new infrastructure, such as a new rail link. Here the landowner may even be willing to volunteer to make payment for all or some of this infrastructure, in cash or in kind because they know that it is they who will most benefit from it. Another is where the state is considering granting planning permission for a development but is deterred from doing so because this would require additional expenditure on its part for new services like roads, schools, health care facilities and so on.

There are wider arguments that everyone, not just landowners, has the right to benefit from the land and natural resources of our planet and that any increase in the value of a plot of land is the result of the activities of the community, both the state and private individuals, not those of its landowner.

The legal position in the UK turns on the Town and Country Planning Act (1947) and subsequent legislation. This Act nationalised the right to develop land and made clear that a land owner has no legal right to any increase in its market value when planning permission is granted. It can be argued that subsequent planning legislation has complicated matters, as the 1947 Act removed any value contributed by the hope of future grant of planning permission from the compensation code for

Compulsory Purchase Orders and thus into expectations of land value, while the 1959 Act re-introduced hope value.

Land value or uplift from specific causes

The rest of this section assumes that there is fairly wide agreement that the community does have some rightful claim on uplifts in land value under certain circumstances. It explores land value uplift from regulatory change, from infrastructure investment and from all other possible causes.

Regulatory change

The windfall gain that accrues to the landowner when planning permission is granted has several consequences. It drives some development – for example it encourages owner-occupiers to develop and, when their property increases in value as the result, they tend to attribute this to their own ingenuity as a developer rather than as a gift from the community. On a larger scale it provides developers with a business model in which they profit more from land value uplift than they do from building and where they are incentivised to bank land that is currently designated as agricultural for future development.

Those who are close enough to see what is happening, yet not so close that they can profit from it, are often strong supporters of an effective method for land value capture – particularly local authorities for whom development otherwise is a matter of acquiring new spending liabilities for roads, social care and so on. Even developers can accept the rationale for paying over some of their land value uplift to a local authority that is going to provide these services.

Infrastructure investment

When the government makes a major investment in new infrastructure, for example, a new rail link, road or broadband, people again often recognise both the increase in land values that occurs and the debt that local landowners owe to the government in return. This is not always welcome; a local resident may well resent any suggestion that they should make any contribution to the cost of a new metro station close to their home on the grounds that they never use it, even though it increases the desirability of their home and so its market value. But this is a minority position, and overall, there tends to be support for land value capture where this arises from spending on well-conceived infrastructure.

All other causes

Land values rise for many other reasons, many of which are invisible to local residents. In addition to regulatory change and infrastructure investment, these include public investment in schools, health care, street lighting, policing, libraries parks and so on. They also result from private investment that improves the neighbourhood including renovation of the fabric and investment in pubs, restaurants, cafés, and other commercial ventures.

Land Value Capture can therefore be appropriately defined as the 'recovery by the public of the land value increments generated by actions other than the landowner's direct investments... primarily on the increment generated by public investments and administrative actions' (Martim Smolka 2013:8). This definition recognises the key role played by the state but also acknowledges the part played by individuals and corporations.

Indeed, the value of an unimproved plot of land, unlike the value of any improvements, is never due to the actions of its owner. So, all land value increase is generated by actions other than the landowners' direct investments. Land Value Capture can, and in a stewardship economy would, encompass collecting the entire land value including but not limited to any recent increase.

Market value or market rent?

The market value of a plot of land or aspect of the environment is the 'estimated amount for which a property should exchange on the date of valuation between a willing seller and a willing buyer in an arms-length transaction after proper marketing wherein the parties had each acted knowledgeably, prudently and without compulsion'. (RICS 2009:42).

The market rent of a plot of land or aspect of the environment is the 'estimated amount for which a property should lease (let) on the date of valuation between a willing lessor and a willing lessee on appropriate lease terms in an arms-length transaction after proper marketing wherein the parties had each acted knowledgeably, prudently and without compulsion' (RICS 2009:42). It is equal to the opportunity cost of leaving vacant land (or unused natural resources) unused.

Both the market value and market rent of land are measures of land value. Which should be captured? We need to be clear about this in order to reach a shared understanding about several important issues including:

- speculation, where market value rises ahead of rising market rents

- hope value, where the market rent reflects the value in current permitted use while the market value includes the hope that planning permission will be granted

- the impact of Land Value Taxation, which reduces market value but not, when paid by the owner rather than by the tenant, the market rent.

It is sometimes expedient to express land value capture as a proportion of (increase in) market value, not least because there is often a windfall capital gain that can provide the means of payment. At other times it is expedient because sources of information are available about sales, and so market values. But market value ultimately depends on future expected market rents (net of land taxes), even when this is distorted in the short run by speculative pressures. There are many reasons why we should be capturing ongoing increases in market rent, not one-off increases in market value:

- Destruction of the land market. As capture approaches 100 per cent, the market value of land falls to zero and transfers of property can no longer be conducted by sale. Rather, the land market needs to consist of offers to pay the market rent of land .

- Erosion of the tax base. Any significant capture of land value will reduce the market value of that land. As capture approaches 100 per cent, the market value of land falls to zero and there is nothing left to capture.

- Hope value. When an owner hopes that their land will in the future be granted planning permission, its market value will rise to reflect this hope value. Its market rent, reflecting its value in current permitted use, will remain unchanged. It is only fair that the owner should be burdened by taxes that reflect the rent they are able to receive not a rent that they might in the future be able to receive if there were permission for other uses.

- Developers' cash flow. The current business model is one in which developers face a long period of initial expenditure during which they acquire land, assemble a sometimes complex site, negotiate planning permission and make Section 106 and CIL contributions and perhaps construct the development before they receive any income from sales or rentals. If site acquisition and land value capture payments all took the form of payments of rent there would be far less risk, indebtedness or need for capital gain rather than construction. Indeed, most of the land value capture would be paid by the occupants and users of the buildings, not the developers and some would be available for long-term maintenance (particularly green spaces). The current risk attached to initial land purchase, calculated using the residual method, would shrink. Local authorities would then lack the necessary cash up front to fund their provision of necessary infrastructure, but they could issue bonds (as with Tax Increment Financing) to be paid from the ongoing Land Value Capture payments.

- Land value capture beyond a defined project. One-off payments related to increases in market value rarely extend beyond the development itself, while uplift in land values may take place further afield. Regular collection of market rents across the whole country ensures that any increase in land values that ripples out will not be omitted.

- Delayed development. Where a one-off charge is levied, particularly related to a property's market value, there is an incentive to delay development until the legislation is withdrawn. Regular payments proportional to market rent are much less easy to avoid in this way.

- Transparency. Where one-off land value capture takes the form of contributions in kind, such as the building of a school or road, the process is usually less transparent, tends to benefit new residents rather than existing local priorities and allow the private sector developers unduly to influence local authority decisions.

- Errors in estimation of uplift. The basis of the market value, even when confirmed by a market transaction, is the discounted sum of future expected market rents. At the point where the development is completed it is easy to make an error in the future expected rents or in the discount rate or in both. It is most accurate to collect those rents year by year rather than try to anticipate them all at the start. It seems likely that rents are initially underestimated and that discount rates, often treated as equal to current interest rates, are set too high. In both cases the amount of land value uplift that is captured is less than it should be.

- Logic. In the long run it is the uplift in the market rent that provides the uplift that can be captured. The logical time to capture the uplift is throughout the whole time when market rents are uplifted.

Ways to capture land value

While land has formed the basis for taxes and tithes since Sumerian times, there are few examples of modern states that raise a large part of their revenue from the land. The only exceptions are Hong Kong and Singapore while others raise at least some revenue through a variety of land value capture approaches.

There are three broad ways in which the value of land can be captured:

- land is owned by a public body (the state or a body acting for the public good)

- uplifts in the value of land are captured as one-off charges or fees

- taxes on the value of land are collected on a regular basis.

Public ownership

State

State ownership of land has potential disadvantages – the pollution of industrial land in Eastern Europe remains a stark reminder. But there are examples of state ownership that have worked well, of which Hong Kong and Singapore provide interesting examples. Here the state's strategy has been to let land on long leases. State ownership of land could have introduced massive inefficiencies, but this has been avoided by the use of market mechanisms to allocate land on medium-term leases to private users.

Hong Kong

The British economic model for its colony in Hong Kong was to retain ownership of all land (apart from the Anglican cathedral) by the Crown, partly because the Crown representative was unable to sell land that he could not be sure would end up being owned by the British Government, but also partly to ensure that the colony was self-financing without being a drain on the British economy or imposing taxes on the residents (Andrew Purves 2015: 7).

Outright ownership of the land allows the state to benefit in many different ways, and a number of approaches have developed in an ad hoc fashion that have changed over time. These have included regular payments of a proportion of the rateable value of the property, such as the General Rates and the Government Rent and taxes on rental property income. In addition, the government is the owner of the Mass Transit

Railway (MTRC), which profits from property rentals and sales around its stations.

But the particular feature of the allocation of land in Hong Kong are the land lease auctions, used to allocate land that has been reclaimed from the sea and land that has been re-zoned and brought in to new uses. These auctions are known locally as land sales, as the tenure is effectively indefinite provided that the general rates and government rent are paid (Andrew Purves 2015: 7, 17, 19, 31, 32). There is an established secondary market in these leases (Sock-Yong Phang 2000:338). Leases granted in the 1970s captured 39 per cent of the increment in land values that occurred between 1970 and 1991 (Sock-Yong Phang 2000:343).

The revenue from leases and regular payments has made possible the regime of low taxes on income and business on which Hong Kong's success is founded. It has served Hong Kong's economy well, although land lease auctions have disadvantages when compared with the regular payments made under a regime of Land Value Taxation. Intermittent payments reflect out-of-date valuations; the purchase price of land is high; residential units are small; income inequalities are great; and, as only small numbers of leases are made available at any time, bidders are able to form cartels that keep prices down.

Singapore

The British did not leave Singapore with a similar legacy of state-owned land, but the post-colonial government has purchased land at agricultural prices and now owns 58 per cent of the land. They lease plots on long leases for housing and commercial use (Andrew Purves 2015: 80). A Housing and Development Board (HDB) assembles land and contracts construction, selling leases to residents. Around 90 per cent of HDB residents are owner-occupiers, though there is some uncertainty about whether the 99 year leases will be rolled over or will revert to the government at the end of their duration (Andrew Purves 2015: 85).

The most successful method of capturing some of the rise in land values that occurs when infrastructure is provided in ownership economies has probably not been through taxation but through ownership and development of land close to infrastructure hubs as in the Hong Kong MTRC described above.

The 19th century American railroad expansion was funded by real estate development. In London, the Country Estates subsidiary of the Metropolitan Railway Company undertook substantial residential development along its lines between the 1880s and 1930s – Metroland – which subsidised the operation of the railway as well as growing their passenger base. Hong Kong's MTRC is financed mainly through developing land at its stations.

The great advantage of this approach is that it is those who benefit from the infrastructure, as demonstrated by the uplift in land value it causes, pay for it. There is no burden of general taxation on people living at a distance from the infrastructure (Fred Harrison 2006a:87).

Charities

Some charities own and manage land in ways that are intended to provide benefits to the public (usually in the form of access) and the environment (in the form of conservation). In the UK the National Trust and the Woodland Trust are examples.

One-off payments

One-off fees and charges have been levied in many countries to capture uplifts in land value. They are paid when some event takes place such as transfer of ownership, granting of planning permission or provision of infrastructure.

Charges of this sort are attractive to tax authorities because the event is easily recognised, it is often associated with a payment or transfer of value out of which the charge can be extracted, and there is no need to value and collect taxes from the whole stock of properties as there is with an ongoing property tax. These advantages of one-off payments, however, need to be contrasted with the benefits of ongoing tax payments.

Voluntary one-off contributions

Where one landowner is the main beneficiary they may be prepared to provide a voluntary subsidy to fund the infrastructure. This is how a lot of development was funded in England in the 19th century – for example the early canals, and the provision of roads in the areas of central London developed by Thomas Cubitt. Olympia and York's self-interest led them down the same route in their planning for Canary Wharf.

Development Land Taxes

Kate Barker (2004:78) identified four times since the second world when taxes on new developments (where the uplift in land values on granting planning permission are an important part of the business model) have failed in the UK. These are: the Development Charge under Clement Attlee in 1947; the Betterment Levy under Harold Wilson in 1967; Development Gains Tax under Ted Heath in 1973/4; and the Development Land Tax under Jim Callaghan in 1976. In each case landowners correctly anticipated that the tax would be removed after a change of government and held potential development land off the market until this took place. In spite of this experience, she recommended a version of exactly this approach, the Planning Gain Supplement, in her review of ways to address future housing needs.

Planning gain and development

Section 106 payments

In the UK Section 106 of the Town and Country Planning Act 1990 allows a developer to enter into a planning obligation with the relevant local authority that might include restrictions, obligations or monetary payments. It has been used by local authorities to capture planning gain. The rationale has been that, if a developer is going to build units such as housing or commercial buildings, it should make a contribution to the expenditure that the local authority will have to make for roads, street lighting, schools, community buildings and so on.

It is an approach that has funded useful development, though the ad hoc nature of the often adversarial negotiations lead to uncertainty for developers, a sense of impotence amongst underfunded planning authorities, dissatisfaction by local residents and high transaction costs for all.

Community Infrastructure Levy

While Section 106 continues to be used for site-specific planning obligations, the Community Infrastructure Levy 2010 was introduced by the Planning Act 2008 to remedy some of the deficiencies of Section 106 such as its uncertainty, unequal burden and lack of transparency. It allows local authorities to raise a levy on developments to fund any associated infrastructure in the wider area. It has proved to be unpopular and ineffective outside areas of high land value such as London.

Land transactions

Both Stamp Duty Land Tax and Capital Gains Tax capture land value when the ownership of land is transferred.

Stamp Duty Land Tax is paid in the UK when a property is sold. Because the liability for tax arises every time the property is sold, it penalises owners who keep their properties for relatively short lengths of time even when this is the most efficient thing to do and leads to owners retaining properties that they think they might perhaps need again at some stage in the future. Taxes on transactions make the land market 'sticky' and the banding structure distorts sale prices.

Capital Gains Tax is paid on disposal of assets where these have risen in value. It has fewer adverse consequences than Stamp Duty Land Tax as it rarely prevents sales from going ahead, but the complexity of the tax with its tapers and allowances means that little of the potential revenue is in fact raised. The most glaring example of this is that a person's primary residence, which for most people is their major financial asset, is exempt from Capital Gains Tax.

Ongoing property taxes

Regular ongoing property taxes have advantages over one-off land value capture. They capture land value uplifts from all causes, not just from a single intervention. Indeed, they provide a source of revenue even when land values are not rising. They ensure that the revenue continues for as long as the development benefits landowners rather than being limited to a single payment that may not be put to best use. Ongoing property taxes do not impose upfront costs on the developer, leaving the ultimate owners to find the revenue from their ongoing profits. And they avoid the transaction costs for both developer and local authority that arise from the need to negotiate, and take to appeal, agreements on a development-by-development basis.

Infrastructure projects have been successfully financed through an annual tax on the value of land affected by infrastructure, for example the irrigation canals of Modesto, Turlock and Stanislaus in California in the 19th century (Fred Harrison 1983: 223). Some property taxes such as these fall only on the properties directly affected. However, property taxes normally fall on all properties including those receiving specific benefits.

Orthodox property taxes

In the UK the two most important ongoing property taxes are the Council Tax for domestic property and the National Non-Domestic (Business) Rates for non-domestic property. The design failings in these two taxes are described below, but both capture a proportion of the value of land.

Property taxes are generally paid on a regular basis in proportion to the market value of the whole property (land plus buildings). Property taxes are a combination of a Land Value Tax, which encourages development, and a tax on artefacts (buildings), which discourages it.

Other drawbacks may arise from the detailed design of the tax, for example, valuations made on the basis of current use not the highest and best use and the wide range of exemptions such as those for derelict buildings in the Non-Domestic (Business) Rates regime.

In spite of the damage done by taxing business assets such as buildings, most property taxes are levied on the value of the whole property because this is the value that is revealed in market transactions whether for sale or rent. Rarely, as in Pennsylvania, a split-rate tax is levied in which the tax on the buildings is lower than the tax on the land, though this requires the valuer to separate the values of these two components. Split-rate taxes are equivalent to a combination of a Land Value Tax with a tax falling on the total value of the improvements.

Voluntary ongoing contributions

A local authority may choose to act on behalf of all local businesses when they can see that this will benefit the local area. Budget airlines in Europe keep their prices down by flying to regional rather than national airports, not least because many of these regional cities are willing to pay them to do so. These cities hope that improved transport links will increase the city's income from business and tourism, which will in turn generate taxes to pay the airline.

The involvement of local businesses can be formalised by agreeing Business Improvement Districts, Tax Increment Financing or a Business Rate Supplement.

Business Improvement Districts

A Business Improvement District (BID) may be proposed by a local authority, a business or a network of business interests. Once the proposal has been made explicit all businesses in the designated area are invited to vote on its adoption. Where the BID is approved, a supplement is added to the National Non-Domestic (Business) Rates of all businesses in the designated area. The income is used, in a way not always transparent, to deliver services to business that are otherwise not being provided.

Tax Increment Financing

Like the Business Rate Supplement and Business Improvement Districts, Tax Increment Financing is a local initiative. Its aim is to finance redevelopment of an area by identifying the increment in local property tax revenue that will arise as the result of the redevelopment, and hypothecating this to fund public sector infrastructure judged to be necessary to unlock the redevelopment itself.

First introduced in California in the 1950s, the usual model is for bonds to be issued, raising capital for the re-development, and for the revenue from the increment in property tax to be used to pay interest and capital on the bonds. Alternatively, the revenue can be spent as it is received, without incurring any debt.

The approach has been generally well received, particularly in America where there is most experience, but it has its critics. Since the increased revenue due to general property price inflation is counted into the increment that is hypothecated for a particular area, other areas in the same tax jurisdiction may be deprived of spending. And some areas have used it to compete with others for inward investment by providing what is a form of tax break.

Business Rate Supplement for Crossrail

The Business Rate Supplement in London, dedicated to providing some funding for Crossrail, is a time-limited 2 pence in the pound supplement on the business rate that is being paid by businesses with a rateable value of more than £55,000 per year, about one in five London businesses. Although this is a compulsory payment it was negotiated in advance with business leaders in London, who could see the benefits that Crossrail would bring to their businesses and the increase in their land values that would result.

Land Value Tax

A Land Value Tax is generally introduced because of its beneficial impact on land use and economic efficiency and will automatically capture the full uplift (or indeed reflect the reduction) in the market rent of land affected by planning consent or infrastructure development. This is automatic, free of cost and requires none of the negotiations that one-off charges require. While betterment charges discourage landowners from putting land on the market, a Land Value Tax encourages them to do so if they are not already making best use of it.

Stewardship fees in a stewardship economy are a particular form of Land Value Tax in which the tax or charge is equal to 100 per cent of the market rent of land. They are paid regularly and unconditionally and depend only on the market rent of the land. The intention is to stimulate the efficient use of land.

Although Kate Barker argued that Land Value Taxation is not an effective way to bring land on to the market, she did describe it as a 'good method of raising revenue without distorting behaviour' that 'may also have a useful role in recapturing for the public purse part of the uplift in land values that can occur as a result of public investment' (Kate Barker 2004:73). Robert Andelson (2000) provides an extensive survey of Land Value Taxation around the world, and Tony Vickers (2007:25-35) provides a succinct summary. Their descriptions include not just conventional Land Value Taxes but also split-rate property taxes where land is taxed more heavily than improvements.

Land Value Taxes were used in many states with a history of British colonial rule including Australia, New Zealand, South Africa, Kenya, Jamaica and Pennsylvania. They arose in Denmark from traditional taxes on the productive capacity of agricultural land, and from there they have spread to the Baltic States. Land Value Tax has also been used in Chile. There is plenty of experience of local taxes of this sort that have been applied at a fairly modest rate - rarely more than 50 per cent of the market rent and usually less than 15 per cent (equivalent to between 2.5 per cent and 0.7 per cent of the market value) (Robert Andelson 2000).

In recent years there has been a move away from Land Value Taxation towards conventional property taxes in several countries, including the removal of the split-rate in Pittsburgh in 2001 (Richard Dye & Richard England 2009:14).

Australia

Australia has seen the most extensive use of Land Value Taxation, where it raised 8.6 per cent of the total taxes in 2005-6 across federal, state and local levels (Tony Vickers 2007: 27). It has, however, been in retreat in spite of its use of sophisticated valuation methods with results that are transparent to the public. This is likely to be in part due to poor design of exemptions and reliefs which bring it in to disrepute and in part to the increasingly powerful lobby by homeowners who recognise, rightly, that Land Value Taxation reduces the financial gain they make from owning a home.

One lesson from Australia is that significant levels of Land Value Taxation can be achieved but that the benefits of the tax have to be made clear to voters, for example by using the revenue for some specific identifiable purpose. Another is that it should be applied to all land with no exemptions or reliefs, as these generate a sense of unfairness.

New Zealand

New Zealand has used Land Value Taxation since the beginning of British colonial rule, and it remains the most common form of local tax. It was popular with local voters and rarely abandoned but when local government was re-organised into larger areas in the 1980s became less used.

Pennsylvania

Split-rate taxes, in which the rate paid on the value of land is three to twelve times higher than the rate paid on the value of buildings, were used in many cities in Pennsylvania. This demonstrably increased regeneration, with a tax shift of 1 per cent from buildings to land, associated with a 16 per cent increase in construction (Plassman and Tideman 1999).

Jamaica

The British introduced Land Value Taxation in Jamaica in 1957, primarily to break up large land holdings and stimulate development, although it was not fully implemented till 1977. It is levied at about 1 per cent of market value for commercial sites and a quarter of this for domestic properties and amounts to about 1 per cent of total tax revenues (Tony Vickers 2007: 34).

Denmark

Denmark's Hartkorn Tax, based on the productivity of agricultural land, was abolished in 1903 and replaced by an income tax. There remained an active interest in Land Value Taxation, and Denmark implemented a Tax on Incremental Land Values from 1933 to 1965.

From 1957 to 1960 a coalition Ground Duty Government implemented a Land Value Tax at the level of municipalities and a Tax on Incremental Land Values at the level of the state. The state level tax was soon repealed but the local tax was implemented at a surprisingly high rate – in Vallensbæk it amounted to a total of 9 per cent of the market value of the land (Ole Lefmann 2017).

Although there have historically been low levels of appeals against valuation, there have been legal challenges that Land Value Taxation is contrary to human rights on the grounds that there are not enough sales of undeveloped land in urban areas to justify the valuations (Tony Vickers 2007: 29). The main lesson from the Danish experience is that, if the general public are not well informed about the benefits of the Land Value Tax, they will not support it.

Estonia

Estonia introduced a Land Value Tax in 1993. This is levied at between 0.5 per cent and 2.0 per cent of market value of land (roughly equivalent to 10-40 per cent of its market rent) with exemptions for owner-occupied properties. However, the land has probably been undervalued (Aivar Tomson 2001:206). The tax provides up to a third of the revenue for local authorities in rural areas, although it amounts to only 1 per cent of national tax revenue (Tony Vickers 2007:30).

UK

In the 20th century there were several attempts to put a Land Value Tax on the statute books in the UK – most famously David Lloyd George's 'Peoples Budget' of 1909 which was defeated in the Lords; Philip Snowden's Labour budget of 1931 which was enacted but repealed by the coalition National

Government; and Herbert Morrison's defeated London Rating (Site Values) Bill of 1939 (Tony Vickers 2007: 21).

Lessons for a stewardship economy

The levels of Land Value Taxes that have been implemented do not challenge the nature of ownership or pose practical challenges to the land market in the way that stewardship fees equal to 100 per cent of the market rent inevitably do. But there are lessons that we can learn from these limited levels of Land Value Taxation and from other ongoing property taxes.

One-off taxes and charges differ in important ways from Land Value Taxation and stewardship. These taxes, which Tony Vickers refers to as dead-end taxes (Tony Vickers 2007: 69), have had 'unexpected' adverse consequences (Owen Connellan 2004:21) and have contributed to public opposition to Land Value Taxation. They, too, provide important lessons about how not to implement a stewardship economy.

Don't tax buildings and improvements

Most property taxes – for example in the UK the old Local Authority Rates, the current Council Tax and the National Non-Domestic (Business) Rates – are levied on the total value of the property, on land plus improvements. It's the easiest and most obvious thing to do as the land and the improvements are normally sold as a unit. This sale provides an unequivocal market valuation for that property and a 'comparable' that can be used when valuing similar properties. But taxing improvements is not economically efficient because it discourages people from developing their sites by constructing and maintaining buildings and other improvements and introduces a deadweight loss of taxation. (See Stewardship Economy book 5 for explanation of deadweight loss)

Tax market rent not current rent

If a tax on land is levied as a proportion of its current rent the owner bears no financial burden when they keep their land idle or in sub-optimal use, commanding little or no current rent. A charge on the market rent, by contrast, is not reduced when the land is kept idle and provides an incentive to put the land to the maximum use consistent with current planning regulations, its highest and best use (HABU). Taxing current use, like taxing improvements, is inefficient as it provides no incentive to make good use of the land and fails to collect all of the available revenue.

Tax ownership not occupation

The liability for property taxes should fall on the owner not the occupier. In practice they are often levied on the occupier, falling only on the owner when a site is unoccupied. It may be difficult to establish who the owner is, particularly when a property is owned by an offshore entity, making it difficult or impossible to collect the tax. It makes little practical difference in most cases, because the incidence of the tax (who bears the ultimate economic burden) always falls on the owner. But taxing the owner makes it clearer that this is not a tax on business activity but on ownership.

The solution to the problem of non-payment of property taxes by the owner is not to make the occupier liable but to apply sanctions for non-payment which might include simply noting the unpaid fees, plus interest, as a charge against the value of the property when sold. An alternative is to make ownership conditional on paying the tax, granting to the tax authority the power to sell the property and recoup any debts owed to it.

Don't tax transfers

The easiest way to tax land is to tax some proportion of its market value (sale price) each time it is bought and sold. In the UK, Stamp Duty Land Tax functions in this way. Capital Gains Tax provides a roundabout way of tapping in to the price rise that most properties enjoy between the time they are bought and the time they are sold. But a tax on property transfers suffers from numerous disadvantages:

- it applies only to sites that change hands each year

- it captures only a small proportion of the year-on-year increase in land values

- it discourages transfers and so makes the land market less efficient

- it penalises those who transfer land, even when the transfer puts it into the hands of someone who will make better use of it

- it rewards people or firms who retain ownership of land over long periods of time even when they are not making good use of it

- it is levied on improvements as well as on land, and so discourages improvement

- it offers opportunities for corrupt and collusive behaviour in which buyer and seller hide some of the price from public view

Stamp Duty Land Tax, though not Capital Gains Tax, penalises people even when their property falls in value.

Don't tax planning gain or development

Even governments with no general enthusiasm for taxing land have tried to capture the rise in land values that occurs at the time when planning permission is granted or development takes place. These are, like taxes on transfers, all examples of one-off taxes.

In South East England, land with planning permission for residential use can have a market value that is hundreds of times greater than that of similar land restricted to agricultural use. If planning permission is granted why should the owner of the land benefit from this windfall rise in value? It is the community that has granted planning permission and the community that has made it a desirable place to live by providing and conserving the local environment, amenities, schools, healthcare, employment, transport links and so on – but the community gets no return on this investment.

More importantly, taxes on development and planning gain have proved to be ineffective. They fail because they delay or block development; cause land prices to rise as land is held off the market; are uncertain, complicated, and incur transaction costs; fail to capture most of the rise in value; and fail to capture rises in value that are brought about for other reasons.

Taxes on planning gain frequently delay development and may even prevent it from taking place at all. Each attempt at taxing development in the UK has frozen the land market and prevented or delayed development. The main reason is that landowners have believed, correctly, that if they withdraw their property from the market the tax would be removed after the next election.

When landowners respond to the imposition of a tax on development by holding their properties off the market, the scarcity of land drives up its price. Taxes on development actually benefit landowners.

Both Section 106 and the Community Infrastructure Levy suffer from the need for the developer to negotiate with the local authority, which adds unnecessary uncertainty and transaction costs to the process of development. It also favours the developers, who are better resourced than the local authority and so better able to make their case, particularly at appeal.

Levying a tax at the point when development occurs is a tempting proposition, as the profit of the developer provides a ready source to fund the tax payment. But, as well as the high transaction costs, it fails to capture most of the rise in the value of development land, let alone the value of land in general.

Agricultural land that may in the future be granted planning permission begins to rise in market value some 15 years before planning permission is granted (Fred Harrison 1983:67). This will be missed by a mechanism that identifies only the rise in value that occurs when permission is actually granted.

Once a development has taken place, the benefits continue long in to the future while taxes on development are usually a one-off charge that fail to capture the ongoing benefit. A tax or charge needs to be levied periodically and indefinitely.

Development land makes up only a small proportion of the total land area and granting planning permission is just one of a whole range of ways in which decisions and expenditure by government, civil society and private enterprise give rise to increases in land value that are captured by landowners.

A Land Value Tax, most effectively one that collects 100 per cent of the market rent as in a stewardship economy, would make it possible to collect the whole of this revenue for the common good. The stewardship fees would rise automatically – not just when planning permission is granted or when infrastructure is provided, but when this is anticipated and from whatever cause.

One of the times when, in an ownership economy, there is a particularly powerful incentive to collect land value uplift is when collection is the factor that can make or break the provision of new infrastructure. The partial funding of Crossrail by the Supplementary Business Rate is a good example of its effective use. But it is a very partial alternative to an ongoing Land Value Tax and requires separate negotiation for each scheme.

Many attempts to tax land, particularly taxes on planning gain and development, have failed because landowners anticipate, correctly, that the tax will eventually be removed. They have a powerful incentive simply to withhold the land from development until that happens. The landowner can anticipate both the increase in land value when the tax is removed and the increase that is anyway likely to have occurred over the intervening time. A tax or charge must be understood to be fair, and it needs to command wide political support. Only in these circumstances is it likely that the tax regime will be sufficiently stable to prevent withholding of land from development.

Apply the same tax rate to all land

Land varies in value, and an acre of high-value land clearly should attract a higher tax than an acre of low-value land. However, it is important that the tax is applied at the same rate, that is to say, the same proportion of the market rent, to all land.

Many examples of 'land taxes' apply a different rate of tax to different sorts of property. This is usually a well-intentioned attempt to ease the tax burden where this seems unfair, but it causes a range of problems and distortions of economic behaviour. A tax or charge should be applied in proportion to the market rent of the land;   whatever it is used for, with no exemptions or exceptions, whether the property is currently in use, whoever uses it and whatever the value of the property. This is necessary both to ensure that the tax system is fair and to encourage efficient land use.

In strict proportion to market rent

Some taxes on land, such as Stamp Duty Land Tax in the UK, are applied at higher rates for properties in higher valuation bands. This introduces a distortion into the prices that people will pay for properties near the margins of the bands.

A fair tax on property should be neither progressive, in the sense of taxing the wealthy at a higher rate than the poor, nor regressive, in the sense of taxing the poor at a higher rate than the rich. It should be in proportion to the market rent. To take one rather extreme example – the Queen pays Council Tax for Buckingham Palace (she is not legally required to do so but does so voluntarily). This property falls in to Band H which, in the borough of Westminster in 2017-18, required payment of Council Tax of only £1376 per year. The market value of the palace was estimated in 2016 to be around £2.2 billion www.foxtons.co.uk/discover/2016/04/how-much-is-buckingham-palace-worth.html, so its Council Tax amounts to only 0.6 per millionth of its market value. At the other end of the scale a Band A property in Weymouth, currently valued at £120,000, pays a Council Tax of £1258 per year – around 1 per cent of its market value. This rate is more than ten thousand times greater than the Queen pays for Buckingham Palace.

Whatever it is used for

Many local property taxes are levied at different rates on different types of property. Sometimes the rate on business and commercial properties is lower, to stimulate business development in the area. Often, as in the UK, it is the rate on residential property is lower than on business and commercial properties. This distorts land use.

The Council Tax is provided with a whole range of exemptions which vary between local authorities, for particular groups of individuals including students, apprentices, carers, diplomats, members of religious communities and the armed forces. Homes left unoccupied by students, carers, prisoners, people moving into a care home or hospital and dwellings that have been repossessed or compulsorily purchased are indefinitely exempt. Discounts of up to 50 per cent may be available, at the discretion of the local authority, for holiday homes, second homes and homes that have been unoccupied for more than six months. There is a 25 per cent discount for homes with a single occupant.

Council Tax depends, therefore, not just on the value of the property but on the number and type of occupants. It is described as a tax on property (land plus buildings) but this dependence on the occupant combined with its regressive nature mean that it is closer to a tax on people than on property - like the Community Charge (Poll Tax) that it replaced in 1993.

National Non-Domestic (Business) Rates exempt, or significantly reduce the rate for a wide range of uses. These include most agricultural land and buildings, parks, places of worship, non-profit organisations, charities, community amateur sports clubs and certain rural businesses like petrol stations and village shops.

While all of these discounts and exemptions may apply to people and organisations that are worthy of collective support, exemptions from property taxes of any sort are not the way to do it . When taxes are applied at different rates to different sorts of land this distorts the allocation of land use. For example, Land Value Taxation has been opposed in New South Wales, understandably enough, as the exemption of farmland from Land Value Taxation has led people to cultivate land that would otherwise be used for conservation (Tony Vickers 2007:27).

Whether currently in use or not

Property taxes may include exemptions for unused land. For example, residential property in the UK may be exempt from

Council Tax if it is unoccupied for up to six months, or twelve months when major repairs are required. In an attempt to tackle criticism of empty homes, the 2017 budget announced that local authorities would have the freedom to charge 100 per cent extra Council Tax on properties that are empty for more than two years. This is unlikely to be high enough to deter wealthy owners from leaving houses empty and does nothing about the first two years.

The National Non-Domestic (Business) Rate exempts industrial and warehouse properties for the first six months that they are empty, and other business premises for the first three months. The rationale is that if the owner is not receiving any rent (actual or notional) they do not have the ability to pay the tax, but the exemption reduces the incentive to minimise these voids.

Longer exemptions are even more unreasonable. The reason that land is not being used, in these cases, is because of a choice made by the owner. This choice may be made because it is economically beneficial to keep land ready to be sold when the price rises, unencumbered by leases or commitments. This demonstrates the complexity of the 'ability to pay' principle – exemptions for land that is underused and could be put to better use are unfair to other taxpayers.

Exemptions for unused land provide little or no incentive to make use of the land and undermine the efficiency of land use that property taxes otherwise promote. Even worse, these exemptions can lead to perverse treatment of improvements. To avoid paying tax, for example, owners may destroy or de-roof buildings to demonstrate that they meet the criteria for the land being 'unused'.

Whoever uses it

Exemptions from tax for particular users of land may be well intentioned but inevitably create unexpected consequences. If charities are exempt, for example, people and organisations will re-arrange their assets so that land is transferred to bodies with charitable status. If the government is exempted, they have little incentive to make best use of their resources (Ronald Coase 1959:21). Exemptions have caused resentment towards land taxes at least since the 10th century when the king in England exempted his favourites from the danegeld (a tax collected to pay off Viking raiders).

Whatever the value of the property

Council Tax provides a particularly unfair illustration of a property tax under which owners of high value properties are taxed at much lower rates than owners of low value properties – even though the inequalities are not generally as marked as those between Buckingham Palace and a low value property in Weymouth. In the UK these inequalities occur both within and between local authority areas.

Within a local authority

In England each property is placed in one of eight bands (A – H) depending on its estimated open market value when it was last valued on 1st April 1991. Each local authority decides an annual Council Tax to be paid by its Band D properties and this determines the Council Tax to be paid by properties in other bands, using the rule of ninths. The highest-value homes (Band H) pay only three times as much as the lowest-value homes (Band A) although they are at least eight times more valuable, making this a highly regressive tax (it takes a higher proportion of the income of the poor than of the rich).

Band	Range of property values at April 1991	Council Tax (Band D = 100%)	Council Tax / mean property value (Band D = 100%)
A	Up to £40,000	67% (6/9)	> 131%
B	£40,001 - £52,000	78% (7/9)	132 %
C	£52,001 - £68,000	89% (8/9)	116 %
D	£68,001 - £88,000	100% (9/9)	100 %
E	£88,001 - £120,000	122% (11/9)	92 %
F	£120,001 - £160,000	144% (13/9)	80 %
G	£160,001 - £320,000	167% (15/9)	54 %
H	More than £320,000	200% (18/9)	< 49%

As the final column shows. Band H homes pay less than half the tax rate on Band D homes,   while Band A homes pay a 30 per cent higher tax rate than Band D homes. The tax is regressive not only between bands but within bands. Taking Band G as an extreme example, properties that were worth £320,000 in April 1991 pay no more Council Tax than those worth £160,001. So, within any local authority area high value properties pay a lower proportion of their value than low value properties.

Between local authority areas

Even more serious is the difference in Council Tax rates between local authorities. About 75 per cent of local authority funding comes from national sources – the Revenue Support Grant (RSG) and a redistributed element of National Non-Domestic

(Business) Rates. The remaining 25 per cent is raised as Council Tax.

The government's original intention when designing the Community Charge (Poll Tax) and its successor was to restrain what it saw as inefficiency and excessive spending by local authorities, by making them accountable for that spending to their electorates. This meant ensuring that a significant proportion of the income of local authorities was raised from local voters. The problem with this approach is that levels of need vary dramatically around the country, and areas of deprivation have both the need for high levels of spending, on social services, for example, and a low tax base with many low-value properties. Both of these factors mean that people in areas of deprivation pay more in Council Tax than those in well-off areas. This imbalance could have been rectified by adjusting the contribution to each local authority by central government, the Revenue Support Grant, to transfer more resources to areas of deprivation.

Billing authority (examples of high and low rates)	Band D House price (2017 Q4) for house worth £78,000 in April 1991 *	Council Tax (2017/8) Band D	Council Tax / Band D house price
Westminster	£471,521	£688	0.0015
Wandsworth	£471,521	£694	0.0015
Kensington & Chelsea	£471,521	£1,062	0.0023
National Average	£297,586	£1,591	0.0053
Sheffield	£223,865	£1,655	0.0074
Salford	£223,865	£1,666	0.0074
Hartlepool	£223,865	£1,833	0.0082
Weymouth & Portland, Dorset	£223,865	£1,887	0.0084

*using Nationwide House Price Calculator

www.nationwide.co.uk/about/house-price-index/house-price-calculator

Residents of relatively poor areas are paying Council Tax at a rate three times greater than residents of affluent areas, even using 1991 valuations and more than five times greater using approximate valuations for 2017. As the result of the variation between local authority areas together with the variation within local authority areas and the regressive impact of the failure to revalue since 1991, the poorest pay Council Tax at more than fifteen times the rate of the richest.

The regressive nature of Council Tax across the country as a whole imposes a deliberate and excessive tax burden on the poorest households. There were over 5 million Council Tax Benefit recipients in England and Wales in 2009-2010, a number greater than those receiving any other means tested benefit. Taking into account the complexity and poor take-up of Council Tax Benefit, it is likely that the figure of those eligible is closer to 8 million (16 per cent of the adult population). These are people driven to means-tested benefits by the tax system which itself fails to raise the necessary revenue from higher value properties.

Tax 100 per cent of market rent

There is a long history of experimental communities that have taken a radical approach to land ownership (Dennis Hardy 1979), including the American Georgist enclaves of Fairhope and the Ardens. Fairhope, a town on the shores of Mobile Bay in Alabama, was founded in 1895 as a 'Single Tax' experiment to put into practice the principle of Land Value Taxation (Charles White Huntington 1922:9).

There are many lessons from the experiences of the Fairhope Single Tax Corporation, as it was called after 1904, one of the most important of which was the reluctance the colonists had in bringing themselves to collect a tax at 100 per cent of market rent. In spite of their rhetoric and intentions, they collected only as much as they felt they needed to meet their obligations to the state and to finance public works. The result was that sales of property came to be accompanied by the payment of a 'bonus'. Consequently, the Corporation was deprived of income, colonists profited from increases in land values; and the Florida land boom of 1925-26 spread to Fairhope (Paul & Blanche Alyea 1956:182).

The radio spectrum auctions, however, provide an example of the collection of 100 per cent of the market rent of a natural resource.

Keep the valuation register up to date
When property taxes are introduced, they are always accompanied by a promise that the valuations will be regularly updated. But this takes a considerable effort, and the longer it is avoided the more politically difficult it becomes. There will be winners and losers from any revaluation, even where it is revenue neutral overall. The cost of upsetting voters who lose from the revaluation outweighs any political benefit, and often prevents the revaluation from going ahead on time (or at all).

If the promises to revalue are not kept, the tax becomes more and more unfair as it relies on increasingly out-of-date valuations and eventually has to be removed. In the UK, for example, the revaluation that would have been required for local authority rates in 1980 was avoided by replacing the rates with the Community Charge (Poll Tax) and Council Tax is still based on valuations carried out in April 1991.

Tony Vickers reports that it has proved possible to carry out annual revaluations in Ohio and in Victoria, Australia, using Geographic Information Systems and Computer Aided Mass Appraisal.

Make valuations & value maps available to the public
Valuation needs to be fair and to be seen to be fair. One way of ensuring this is to make all valuations freely available to the public, and to display the information on colour-coded maps linked to a database as a Geographic Information System (www.landvaluescape.org). The public can make sense of these maps and recognise whether differences in valuations in a local area reflect genuine differences in market rents. This visibility also reduces the scope for corruption in the valuation process.

Anticipate resistance if tax rates are increased

The experience of more than a century of attempts to put Land Value Taxation into place suggest even when property owners allow the introduction of low levels of Land Value Tax they successfully resist increases in the rate of tax, delay the necessary revaluations and eventually force the removal of the tax. Experience from around the world suggests that low levels of taxation of land can be introduced relatively easily, but that beyond this the political power of landowners thwarts the reform.

Don't be surprised if it is complicated

The implementation of any tax is inevitably complicated, as it has to accommodate a very wide range of individuals and circumstances. Income tax is a simple concept, but the implementation of an income tax requires detailed planning and accommodation to a range of circumstances. A tax on the market rent of land should be much simpler, but it will still need a great deal of detailed planning.

Lessons learned

There are lessons to be learned from past experience of taxing land. Charges and taxes on land require long-term stability of the tax regime, regular revaluations, openness and transparency, a tax rate that is a uniform percentage of market rent with no exceptions, freedom from any tax on the value of improvements and valuations based on the highest and best use. Above all, it requires an electorate that understands its beneficial impact on land use and the economy.

Many of the problems that can be anticipated around the introduction of a stewardship economy are not problems of stewardship in itself, but problems of unravelling an ownership economy and the complexities of its tax-benefit system. Stewardship requires the collection of 100 per cent of the market rent of land, and no charge or tax has ever been applied to land at this rate.

Part II How land is valued in an ownership economy

The 'gold standard' way to put a price on anything, including a plot of land, is to expose it to the open market. Anything else is an approximation.

Professional valuers have extensive experience of making judgements about property values in ownership economies, without needing to put a property on the market. They are able to separate the value of a property into the value of the land and that of the improvements. And they can handle the tricky allocation of the value amongst a number of different interests, for example a hierarchy of leaseholds, though this can be very challenging.

Property valuation has, however, from time to time, had a justifiably bad press in the UK. The valuations carried out for Council Tax banding were carried out on a 'drive-by' basis. And there is a widespread belief that values of buy-to-let properties in the years leading up to 2008 were deliberately, and perhaps fraudulently, inflated to allow excessive borrowing.

The valuation of a new building, rather than a property comprising land and buildings, ought to be a more exact business. A quantity surveyor has to rely on professional judgement, but this is based on evidence of the cost of building components, wages and recent tender prices.

Part II prepares for a discussion of the assessment of stewardship fees (Part III) by discussing the methods that are applied to the assessment of land value in ownership economies (RICS 2009 & Ted Gwartney 1999:10). This part also includes a chapter on how the total market rent of the UK can be estimated.

Chapter 3   Valuing property (land plus buildings) in an ownership economy

This chapter begins by exploring the meanings of 'value' and how these differ from the meaning of 'price'. It then discusses the gold standard for establishing the value of any property – the price that it exchanges for in a free and open market transaction. Finally, it considers two of the main approaches that are used in ownership economies to establish the value of a property when it has not itself been recently exposed to the open market.

One of these valuation approaches, **the market or sales comparison** approach, uses market information by comparing the (index) property to be valued with comparable properties that have recently been exchanged in the free market.

Another valuation approach, **the income approach**, provides a way to establish the market value of a property when its market rent is known, or to establish the market rent of a property when its market value is a given.

A third valuation approach, **the cost or Depreciated Replacement Cost approach**, treats separately the values of land and improvements. It is discussed in Chapter 4.

Valuation of land in a stewardship economy (Part III) uses the principles of all these methods of valuation, within the context of a New Land Market.

Price and Value

Price and value have different meanings and groups of specialists use the terms in a variety of ways.

Language

In general (non-specialist) use, the meanings of words are not tied irrevocably to specific definitions. This allows new situations and understandings to be described using existing language, and new understandings to be explored using metaphor. In specialist use, particularly in science, words have very specific meanings. The word 'land', for example, has a different meaning in the specialist languages of geography, surveying, economics and law and this poses challenges in books such as this that straddle many specialist disciplines. Price and value are particularly problematic.

Price

A price is a sum of money that is paid by a recipient to a supplier when something is transferred not by bequest or gift but in an open market transaction. Prices are denoted in money terms.

This definition requires agreement about what an open market transaction comprises – for example the Royal Institute of Chartered Surveyors describes it as an 'exchange between a willing seller and a willing buyer in an arms-length transaction after proper marketing wherein the parties had both acted knowledgeably, prudently and without compulsion'. But such is the overlap in the use of the terms 'price' and 'value' that this quotation is actually taken from their definition of 'market value' (RICS 2009: 42).

Value

Adam Smith (1776: Book 1, Chapter 4) points out that the term 'value' has two quite different meanings. One, which he calls 'value in exchange', is the power something has when purchasing other goods and is synonymous with 'price'. The other, 'value in use', is a measure of utility, of how much we value something. Value in use is a subjective assessment and is expressed not in money terms but as a subjective sense of worth.

Adam Smith identified what has become known as the 'paradox of value' – that things with the greatest value in use, such as water, generally have little value in exchange while things that have a low value in use, such as a diamond, may have a high value in exchange. Neoclassical economics was able to illuminate this by clarifying that value in use is determined by utility while value in exchange is determined by marginal utility.

We have somehow come to equate the price of something (its value in exchange) with the subjective value that we place on its intrinsic value (value in use). Particularly pernicious is the way that the most useful, valuable, workers (caring for others, growing food, dealing with sewage and other refuse) are amongst the lowest-paid in our society. Because their work has low value in exchange they are generally treated as less valuable members of society than those whose work has the highest value in exchange.

It would be logical to use 'price' to refer to value in exchange and 'value' to value in use. This book stays with both the general usage and the specialist language of chartered surveyors and uses 'value' to refer to a 'price', denoted in money terms.

Valuation

Part of the reason why surveyors use the term 'value' rather than 'price' is that one of their important functions is to use their professional skills to estimate the price for which a property would exchange if it were put on the market – the 'estimated amount for which a property should exchange on the date of valuation'. 'Value' here is used to mean 'estimated price'.

Bases of value

The Royal Institute of Chartered Surveyors describes a basis of value as a statement of the assumptions that underlie a valuation. The bases of value that are in most frequent use are the market value and its near relative, fair value, market rent and the investment value (or worth).

Market value

The market value of a property is the 'estimated amount for which a property should exchange on the date of valuation between a willing seller and a willing buyer in an arm's length transaction, after proper marketing and where the parties had each acted knowledgeably, prudently and without compulsion ' (RICS 2009:42).

If a property (or unimproved site) has not recently had its price determined in an open market transaction, the closest approximation to that price is a surveyor's opinion or appraisal of its 'market value' – the price that can reasonably be expected to be achieved assuming that:

- the property is freely exposed to the market
- a reasonable time is allowed for negotiation, taking account of the nature of the property and the state of the market
- values will remain static during that period
- no account is taken of higher bids from special purchasers or tenants.

The 'market rent' is similarly defined, as the rent that can reasonably be expected to be achieved under the same assumptions.

The key ingredients of market value are that the transaction involves the transfer of ownership in an open market between unconnected parties and reflecting the potential of its Highest and Best Use (HABU). It includes hope value where this is present.

Hope value

Hope value is the value conferred by the prospect of development even where there is currently no provision for development. It is not a basis for valuation but may contribute to the market value.

Hope value may contribute to the market rent of a site if the payment of the rent ensures that the lessee maintains security of tenure up to and including the time when development takes place.

Fair value

Fair value is defined as the 'price that would be received to sell an asset in an orderly transaction between market participants at the measurement date' (RICS 2009).

If there is evidence of the market value from recent market transactions for comparable properties, this will provide the basis for estimating fair value. If not, fair value may be based on the Depreciated Replacement Cost.

Market rent

The 'market rent' of a plot of land or aspect of the environment is the 'estimated amount for which a property should lease (let) on the date of valuation between a willing lessor and a willing lessee on appropriate lease terms in an arm's length transaction after proper marketing and where the parties had each acted knowledgeably, prudently and without compulsion' (RICS 2009:42).

The market rent clearly depends on the provisions, particularly the duration, of the lease. (For the purposes of stewardship, which provides indefinite security of tenure provided the stewardship fees (reassessed each year) are paid, the lease duration is indefinite.)

Investment value (worth)

The investment value (worth) is 'the value of an asset to a particular owner or prospective owner for individual investment or operational objectives'.

Direct observation of an open market sale

An open market provides a means of quantifying the price, and so the market value, of plots of land when their ownership is transferred. Price depends on the levels of supply and demand. The interplay between supply and demand is dynamic, though it is often described as an equilibrium.

Demand, in the economic sense, reflects not just the desire to have or to use something but the ability to pay for it. It depends on the subjective value judgements of potential users of the land – either the satisfaction (utility) they would derive from using it or the revenue that they imagine they could earn by employing it for any of a large number of possible uses.

The only person who can truly make this judgement is someone who is actually considering bidding for the land. The market value of land is the highest price that anyone is prepared to pay.

The market value of land may be indirectly assessed by asking people what they would be willing to pay, but there is no way of knowing whether they would actually commit themselves to paying these prices.

Observing the price at which a plot of land is bought and sold in an open market transaction provides a direct way to establish its value that cannot be contested. An open market transaction requires that information be freely available about the sale and about the land. It also requires a mechanism that allows enough time for all bidders to make their maximum offer.

People, including professional surveyors, may have an opinion about what a site is worth, just as they may have an opinion about what a second-hand car or a painting by an old master is worth. But this estimate will rarely be exactly equal to the price at which an open market transaction is actually made.

And although a market sale price should provide the gold standard of market value there are times when it does not do so because the sale is not arms-length, perhaps because there is a special relationship between buyer and seller or because one party has failed to act knowledgeably, prudently or without compulsion. In such cases the market price provides no guide to the market value.

A sale is most transparent when it occurs at auction. A similar result can be achieved when an estate agent acts as a trusted third party, publicises a guide price and adjusts this upwards or downwards according to the offers they receive while keeping all the bidders fully informed.

Direct observation of an open market rent

There are not many places where the current market rent for a property is known as the direct result of observing an open market transaction, for several reasons:

- While most market transactions relating to leasehold properties establish their market rent, owner-occupied properties are offered for sale not for rent and this establishes their market value. Their market rent can be calculated only by making assumptions about how much rent the property would yield.

- Market transactions provide a snapshot of the value of the property at one instant in time. The value of a site some years ago is not, on its own, much help in assessing its value now.

- Some properties are only rarely exposed to the market. This applies to property owned by the state, to commercial sites that form part of a business and to estates and homes, some of which may not have been exposed to the market since 1086.

- Information may be incomplete, incorrect or missing, and even transactions recorded by the land registry may not have taken place in an open market.

- Most properties that are bought and sold comprise both land and improvements rather than unimproved sites. For these properties even an open market transaction cannot directly establish the value of the land alone. This challenge is discussed in Chapter 4.

Valuation by *comparison* - The 'market value'

Valuation by comparison, also known as open market sales comparison, is carried out formally by comparing the index site (the one that is being valued) with other identical or similar sites for which price information is available. The values of these 'comparables' are derived directly from market transactions, and the whole approach is made transparent by providing a list of comparables, their values and the reasons why they were chosen. Small differences between properties can be adjusted for, but separate comparisons need to be made for different types of property use and for sales or rentals.

'Valuation by comparison' is valid only if there are a sufficient number of sites that are comparable with the index site and whose value has been established in the open market in the recent past. In addition to factors that make sites not strictly comparable, a number of things may make comparison difficult or impossible including the lack of recent market information, and the special case of properties in which there are multiple interests.

Recent market information

There are times when no market valuations of any properties are available for comparison. In Russia valuation by comparison was not possible in 1992 as no market-determined rents or prices had been determined in the communist economy.

Even where there is a free market in land, as mentioned above, there are types of land that may never (or infrequently, or only as part of a larger transaction like a merger or take-over) come onto the market. This may be because they are large (e.g., landed estates), complicated (e.g., a railway network) or unique (e.g., the site of a harbour, chemical plant, airport or mine).

Factors influencing the sale price

Estate agents routinely advise that the most powerful determinant of the value of a property is its location. Southerners visiting the north of England have been heard to say, 'that house would be worth a fortune in London', and there is similar geographical variation in the value of commercial, retail and industrial sites.

For the purposes of the taxation of land, valuation by comparison has often been standardised and based on area, street frontage or some other similar measure of size.

The price of land may differ dramatically between adjacent neighbourhoods – location is very finely grained. A comparable site should be similar to an index site in the physical, social and economic characteristics of the site itself and its surroundings. Factors that influence demand for land, and therefore its value, include:

- Restrictions on use
  - planning restrictions
  - easements and covenants.
- Physical aspects of the site
  - topography, orientation, soil fertility, soil pollution, microclimate
  - liability to flooding.
- Location - Physical environment
  - light, views, privacy, surrounding properties and the local built environment, street lighting, access to parks, open spaces, river frontage, sea
  - noise, traffic, air pollution, smells.
- Location - Social environment
  - population density
  - safety, security
  - social factors that are negative or thought to be negative such as proximity to a prison or psychiatric hospital
  - cleanliness
  - proximity to employment
  - proximity to shops, sports facilities and cultural sites
  - school catchment area.
- Location - Economic environment
  - economic usefulness of the site
  - proximity to similar or related businesses
  - connection to services (water, drainage, sewage, gas, electricity, telephone)
  - access to transport (local roadways, car parking off site, motorway, rail, river, canal, sea)
  - state of the local economy, availability and cost of labour and skills
  - proximity to local markets
  - insurance costs
  - levels of taxation.

Requirements for comparables

The factors identified above mean that a site that is used as a comparable for valuation purposes must be similar in, at the very least, socio-economic environment, size, permitted use, planning restrictions, easements, covenants and privileges.

Socio-economic environment

A comparable site needs to be located in the same, or a similar, socio-economic environment. A business must convey the right impression to its clients, people want to live in an area where there are 'people like us'. Danny Dorling has said that house price differentials are a measure of how afraid people are of their neighbours (Danny Dorling 2011).

Size

An ideal comparable site has the same area as the index site. Where this is not the case, sites of different size may be used as a proxy.

For large plots of land, for example agricultural or industrial land, the market rent may be roughly proportional to the area of the plot. For residential land the value is more likely to be related to the possible number of dwelling units that it could accommodate. And for retail premises the value may be related to the length of the frontage, perhaps in combination with area. But whatever scale factor is used to relate the value of plots of different sizes can only be an educated guess that reflects the thinking of prospective buyers

Estimating market value

To estimate the market value of a property using the investment or income capitalisation approach it is necessary to estimate both the market rent of the property and the average yield for similar properties. The valuer needs to establish comparables for both market rent (requiring an active rental market) and yield (requiring an active market for sales), as well as estimating the landlord's expenses.

Permitted use and planning restrictions

Any planning restriction may reduce the market rent of the land to which it is applied. Valuation by comparison requires the use of comparables that are subject to identical planning restrictions. This is easier in countries, like the USA, in which planning is handled through zoning regulations which identify permitted uses in each zone rather than those, like the UK, in which planning applications are dealt with on a site-by-site basis.

Easements, covenants and privileges

In the same way that planning restrictions reduce land values so too do easements, rights of way and a whole range of covenants, conditions and restrictions. Finding comparable sites with the same restrictions, or making a financial allowance for these, may be a serious challenge.

Some sites have associated privileges, for example access to communal gardens or fishing rights, which also need to be taken into account when selecting comparables.

Multiple interests

Many properties are held through a hierarchy of leaseholds and other contracts. A property may have, say, a freeholder (who in the UK holds the freehold from the crown) and holders of long-term (99 - 999 year) and medium-term (25-99 year) leases as well as a variety of short leaseholds, under-leases, sub-leases, tenancies and licences. There may be legally enforceable timeshare rights.

Each interest has impacts on the value of other interests, and these change over time as leaseholds expire. All of these factors make it difficult to assign values accurately. But it is usually possible to make a good-enough estimate. The value of each of these interests can be determined by observation in an open market transaction, or by comparison if it is possible to find comparables with similar terms and duration.

The market value of the whole site is, in principle, the sum of the various interests in it. But the value of a combined freehold and leasehold interest in a property may be greater than the sum of the values when these are held by different parties. This 'marriage value' arises in part from the ability of the leaseholder who is also a freeholder to grant themself a lease extension.

In practice it may be even more complicated than this. There may be other claims on a property that affect its value but cannot be assigned any monetary value. These include shorthold tenancies that prevent re-assignment or sub-letting; the conditional right of a mortgage lender which only comes into play if the person who has taken out the mortgage defaults on the loan payments; mortgages; rights of way; clawback agreements; leasehold reform rights; rights of pre-emption; easements and so on.

Proportional valuation

One method that surveyors may use to make use of near-comparables is by referring to a 'standard site' in a particular area. A housing site that is slightly more desirable than the standard site is assessed to have a value that is proportionally higher than the average site by a few percentage points, for example. Local informants are usually keenly aware of a wide range of factors that make one site more desirable than another. Proportional valuation allows market transactions of near-comparable sites to be translated into a change in the value of the standard site, and thus into the values of all sites that are near-comparables.

The limitations of valuation by sales comparison

There are some large housing estates, or uniform agricultural areas or business parks, where comparables can be identified quite easily. But finding perfect comparables for sites, and particularly finding enough comparables that have recently changed hands, is rarely possible. Most sites are significantly different from their neighbours, and 'comparables' are really 'near-comparables'.

Computer-assisted mass appraisal (CAMA)

Automated Valuation Models are widely used to assess the value of large numbers of properties. These are an approach to valuation by comparison in which, as with assessment of an individual property, the relative values of properties are compared taking account of the multiple factors that determine property value.

These factors are identified by multiple regression analysis or, as geographical data rarely has the independence between variables that this requires, geographically weighted regression (Tony Vickers 2009: 57) and combined in a hedonic pricing model (see Glossary). Such a model draws on information about the index and comparable properties (which may be limited to location and house size but in some North American jurisdictions may include up to 100 factors) (Tony Vickers 2009: 60).

CAMA consists of the valuation for tax purposes of large number of properties in which valuation is informed by an Automated Valuation Model. The appraisal may be of the total property value, or it may be broken down into the values of the land and the buildings, depending on the nature of the underlying model (Tony Vickers 2007:14).

The validity of CAMA depends on the establishment in the market of the sale price of comparable properties as well as the validity of the underlying model. In the USA Automated Valuation Models have been found to provide valuations that are more statistically valid than individual property appraisals, and the use of mapping and isovalue lines enable land values to be assessed more easily and accurately than building values (Tony Vickers 2009: 65).

CAMA was first used in the UK in the Northern Ireland domestic revaluation of 2006-7. It resulted in only 600 appeals, and in 92 per cent of these cases the CAMA valuation was found to lie within 10 per cent of the assessed value (Tony Vickers 2009: 54).

The investment, or income capitalisation, approach

The investment approach is a way of calculating the value of an asset from a knowledge of the revenue it generates. The same logic can be used to calculate the expected revenue from an asset of known value.

The investment approach can take the form of the discounted cash flow approach or of the capitalisation (income multiplier) approach, depending on way that market participants generally assess how much to bid for a site.

Discounted cash flow

A financial asset, such as land, has a market value (asset value or sale price) because its owner anticipates that it will generate an income stream of rent into the future. The market value is equal to the value today of the income stream anticipated in the future, discounted to today's value (the Net Present Value).

The rent is capitalised by multiplying the anticipated payment for each future year by an appropriate discount factor that is often shaped by the nominal interest rate over the intervening years, although in practice it is another variable that has to be estimated by observing the market and summing this series of discounted payments.

Capitalisation (income multiplier) approach

This approach is simpler than the discounted cash flow approach but less flexible. It is used for equities and bonds, where the relationship between value and revenue is known as the price: earnings ratio, as well as real estate.

Investors assume that they will be able to recover the capital value of their investment at any time in the future by putting it on the market. They anticipate that they will each year receive a return on their investment that is related to the price of that investment by a factor known as its 'yield':

Yield = Return on investment/Price of investment

So, in the case of real estate:

Market value = Net market rent/Yield

where the market rent is net of all landlord's expenses, that is to say, it is equal to the net operating income or net income before taxation.

Since Market Value/Net market rent is the number of years it would take to recoup the purchase price, the inverse of Yield is known as the Years' Purchase (YP), income multiplier, capitalisation rate or 'cap rate'.

So, what determines the yield? In a world of rational economic actors, an asset should generate a yield that is at least as much as would be derived from investing its value at the commercial rate of interest for a safe asset. The yield on any investment will be greater than this by a premium that reflects how risky the investment is, and this is generally observable in the market. So, the yield on property is likely to be somewhat higher than the yield on government bonds.

Speculation

The market value may in practice be greater than expected from the market rent, and the yield therefore lower. One reason is that there may be a speculative element to the market value of a site, even when it is determined by an open market transaction. If land prices are rising and are expected to continue to rise, the sale price will reflect this additional expected gain. So, purchase prices are influenced by speculative expectations of future prices as well as by current and expected future market rents and interest rates.

Another reason for higher market values is that the owner may derive satisfaction, utility, from simply holding and enjoying the asset. This is particularly evident in the case of farmers, and the owners of landed estates, whose attitudes are shaped by a sense of duty to care for the land and the wish to pass their holding on to their heirs intact, without requiring a high yield.

Estimating market rent

It is possible to use the converse of the relationship between rent and value to estimate the market rent of a property:

Net market rent = Market value*Yield

or:

Market rent = (Market value*Yield) + landlord's expenses

It is important to remember, however, that it is the market rent that determines the market value not the other way around.

Valuation for Land Value Taxation

When valuing for Land Value Taxation in an ownership economy, the task is to determine the value of plots of land without including the value of the buildings or improvements on it. A plot of land may be completely undeveloped and have been recently exposed to the open market, either for purchase or rent, in which case its value (sale price or rent) has been established

Comparison with undeveloped land

It is possible to use valuation by comparison, using as comparables other undeveloped sites that have recently been exposed to the market. The challenge, however, is that, particularly in urban areas, there are very few undeveloped sites to use as comparables as most land has been developed; and those that are to be found are often not exposed to the market for decades at a time . Even in rural areas most agricultural land is not 'undeveloped' – there are always improvements that rightfully belong to the tenant or landowner.

Land values vary in a very fine-grained way, from street to street in urban areas. Comparables do need to be genuinely comparable, and this means that there need to be plenty of them.

The impact of the lack of true comparables can be minimised by the use of sophisticated modelling techniques that use hedonic pricing models to take account of the many factors that influence land value combined with CAMA. One challenge for this approach is the large number of sites for which information needs to be available in order to construct the hedonic models in the first place. And it still needs undeveloped comparables.

Where there are few undeveloped comparables

The lack of undeveloped comparables is a serious problem for the whole legitimacy of Land Value Taxation. In Denmark there were appeals against the principle of land-only tax assessments on the grounds that there are too few transactions of undeveloped land in urban areas to provide valid comparisons (Tony Vickers 2007: 29).

Where there are not enough comparable unimproved sites Nicolaus Tideman has proposed that assessors could purchase parcels of land with obsolescent improvements, demolish the improvements and auction the land (inviting bids for market rent not market value) (Nicolaus Tideman 2004: 29). This may seem rather extreme, but a small number of these transactions could be financed within the workings of the tax system. Indeed, given the relatively high cost of retrofitting existing homes for carbon-neutrality, demolition may become a more common option in the housing market.

This chapter has described how, in an ownership economy, the best approach to valuation of a property is for its market value (i.e., price) or the market rent to be established in an open market transaction.

Surveyors may be able to assess the market value or the market rent of an unimproved site by comparison with other unimproved sites that have recently come on to the market, but this requires professional judgement and detailed knowledge of comparables.

As an alternative to valuing land directly, either in an open market transaction or by comparison with undeveloped sites, there are ways to separate out the value of buildings and land. Chapter 4 describes the cost approach that is used in ownership economies. It is an accepted approach though in this context generally regarded as a method of last resort.

Chapter 4   Valuing land (and not buildings) in an ownership economy

This chapter describes how the value of land can be established in an ownership economy even where there are no comparable sites that are unencumbered by buildings or other improvements. This situation arises either if all comparable sites have been developed or if there is no market in sites of this type.

The cost, or Depreciated Replacement Cost, approach provides an estimate of the 'value in use' rather than 'value in exchange' of a property. It is a well-established approach that can provide a fair value of a property, though it is considered to be a method of last resort to be used only where there are no comparables available for cost comparison. Its importance is that the approach, applied in a different way, is exactly what is needed for valuation in a stewardship economy (Chapter 6).

The other approach described in this chapter is the Profits or Receipts and Expenditure approach. Here the market rent of a site is estimated on the basis of the net revenue that could be achieved on the site, assuming that it is put to its Highest and Best Use (HABU). This approach includes the Residual method, by means of which the market rent of undeveloped land may be estimated by imagining its possible uses.

The Cost / Depreciated Replacement Cost approach

The Depreciated Replacement Cost is the 'current cost of reproduction or replacement of an asset, less deductions for physical deterioration and all relevant forms of obsolescence and optimisation' (RICS 2009). It is used to value assets that are never normally exposed to the open market. The valuation is used as an entry in the balance sheet of its owner and provides an estimate of 'value in use' not 'value in exchange' (Frances Plimmer & Sarah Sayce 2006).

Once buildings have been erected, they are always bought and sold or leased along with the land on which they stand, so these market transactions cannot put a separate value on buildings and land. The assumption that underlies the cost approach is that the value of a property is equal to sum of the values of the land and the buildings on it. This is a simplifying assumption that can be challenged but is good enough to provide the basis for valuation in both ownership and stewardship economies. Where there is no market in comparable unimproved sites it is possible to put a value on the land element by subtracting the current value of the improvements from the sale price of the property as a whole.

The cost approach is widely regarded as a method of last resort in ownership economies, in part because the price of production of the property (cost of land + price of construction) bears no constant or measurable relationship to the market value of the property. This is a significant problem in ownership economies, but fortunately is not relevant in a stewardship economy where the Depreciated Replacement Cost is not used to estimate the Market Value of a property but used in an entirely different way (Chapter 7).

Separating land from buildings

Separating the value of the buildings from that of the land is not simple. The International Accounting Standards Board does instruct valuers, in the standard IAS7, to apportion the value of a leased asset into two parts, labelled 'land' and 'buildings', the sum of which (by definition) makes up the whole. IAS7 does not, however, define 'land' and 'buildings'. The RICS proposes that 'land' is best defined as the location, the physical ability and the legal right to use and construct improvements on the site, elements that do not depreciate over time; while 'buildings' include physical structures, sunk finance and developer's profit – a wasting asset.

While the Royal Institute for Chartered Surveyors (RICS) does accept the separation of land and buildings by IAS7 in practice in the UK, it points out that it is possible to argue that value relies on other factors such as architectural merit, lease structure, covenants and sunk finance costs – and that the parts do not necessarily add up to the whole (RICS 2006:7). The RICS believes that it is possible to allocate reliably the rent to each element (land and buildings) where the lease is for a self-contained plot of land and a building upon it – provided that there is an active market for land for similar developments in the locality. However, it takes the view that in more complex situations, for example where a lease is part of a multi-let building with no identifiable land attributable to a particular lease, reliable allocation may be impossible (RICS 2009:68).

(While this may be the case in an ownership economy, a stewardship economy provides a practical way to apportion the value of a property between land and buildings even in these complex situations (Chapter 7)).

But to value land using the Depreciated Replacement Cost approach the first question is: 'how do you value the improvements independently of the value of the property as a whole?'

Valuing buildings - the Depreciated Replacement Cost

The Depreciated Replacement Cost is the 'current cost of replacing an asset with its modern equivalent asset less deductions for physical deterioration and all relevant forms of obsolescence and optimisation' (RICS 2009). It is, once again, a method that relies on comparison, but in this case comparison with a hypothetical modern equivalent.

If a building is brand new, its value can be taken to be the actual cost of construction - the Replacement Cost. If it is several years old, its value can be taken to be equal to the Replacement Cost reduced by an allowance for depreciation, the Depreciated Replacement Cost (RICS 2006:13).

Replacement

The improvements

If the building, structure or other site improvements are reasonably modern and likely to be replaced by a virtually identical structure, the replacement building is taken to be to the same as the present one. The surveyor needs to inspect the building to assure themself that the original building work was properly carried out, because if there is unsatisfactory work this reduces the improvement value. They also need to check that the appropriate certificates of completion have been obtained to demonstrate that the work complies with the building regulations and planning permission.

If the building is older, and a modern structure of identical capacity or usable floor space would cost substantially less than an identical replacement, or indeed if modern processes require less space, the modern structure that will serve its purpose is used as the basis for valuation.

Listed buildings (Chapter 7) (of historic or architectural interest) cannot be valued by comparison with equivalent modern buildings, as they are required to be rebuilt with costly replica materials. The replacement cost needs to reflect this and building costs may be difficult to estimate if a building was constructed using a technique no longer in current use.

The replacement should take into account factors that add to the prestige and attractiveness of the building, but not necessarily reproduce each feature in a like-for-like manner.

To establish the Depreciated Replacement Cost of a property in an ownership economy it is also necessary to estimate the value of the site. Where a site is no longer appropriate, for example because it is too expensive, too large or because business requirements have changed, the value of a modern equivalent site is used. This is not relevant to valuation for stewardship, where it is the value of the buildings in isolation from the land for which a Depreciated Replacement Cost is estimated.

The replacement cost

Building costs can generally be estimated by a quantity surveyor, who has experience of recent market prices of the building components and tender prices for similar recently-constructed buildings. If the original costs are available these can be adjusted using industry cost indices. If the original drawings and bills of quantities are available these can be costed using current prices.

The replacement cost is thus based on current building costs, that is to say it allows for the inflation in building costs since the building was constructed. Building costs will be higher in some areas than in others, depending particularly on geographical variations in wage rates. The costings should be notionally backdated so that building costs are those appropriate to a construction ready for occupation at the date of valuation.

Incidental fees (professional fees, acquisition costs, interest charges, VAT where not recoverable but in an ownership economy not the developer's profit) are to be included in the cost of construction.

Subsidies (e.g., Regional Development Grants) should be ignored.

Depreciation

Depreciation for the purposes of financial reporting refers to an allowance made to reflect the consumption of an asset over an accounting period. For the purposes of valuing a building it has a quite different meaning – the reduction in the value of a modern equivalent building that would reflect the actual disadvantages of the index building.

How cars and caravans depreciate

Touring caravans can be thought of as homes that can be bought and sold without a site. They depreciate rapidly in value during the year following their initial sale, reach half their sale value after about seven years and a quarter of their sale value after another seven years (Caravan Price Guide).

Most cars depreciate, like caravans, and are eventually scrapped. But some cars become valued collectors' items – classic or 'cherished'. In a similar way most buildings are eventually demolished, but the value of some buildings rises as their design and features become more highly appreciated.

Physical obsolescence (deterioration)

The degree of physical obsolescence or deterioration that a building suffers depends both on the original design and construction and on the level of maintenance that has been carried out. There is therefore a degree of predictability in the development of physical obsolescence.

One approach to quantifying the loss of value from physical obsolescence is to subtract from the replacement cost a sum that represents an allowance for incurable structural defects, an estimate of the cost of refurbishment to 'as new' appearance and an allowance for the higher maintenance costs and reduced efficiency of an older building. Another approach is for the surveyor to make a judgement of the useful life remaining in the building, at the time of valuation. The Royal Institute for Chartered Surveyors suggests that a valuer should be able to classify a building according to its expected lifetime into one of three categories – less than 20 years, 20-50 years and over 50 years. They can then express this as a percentage of the total (predicted) economic life of the building, and this figure may be taken to be the percentage depreciation.

Functional obsolescence

The building may be worth even less than is apparent from the extent of physical deterioration, because of changes in way that the property can be used – functional obsolescence. If a factory building is suitable only for producing goods for which there no longer any demand or using outdated processes, if holiday makers prefer self-catering accommodation to holiday camps, if a house is located in an area of high crime and vandalism, if a small shop could be profitably replaced by a multi-storey block, if a care home requires refurbishment to comply with the Care

Standards Act – in these situations the value of the building will be less than it would appear from inspecting their fabric.

Assessing obsolescence

Assessing physical obsolescence requires extensive experience and judgement, and assessing functional obsolescence is even more difficult.

It would appear from the figures given for touring caravans that these depreciate exponentially. Valuers sometimes use the working assumption that buildings, too, depreciate exponentially (reducing balance) though over a longer time-scale. Or they may assume that buildings depreciate in a linear way over their lifetime, which is simpler but less realistic.

A more realistic assumption is the S-curve, in which buildings at first depreciate rapidly, then slowly, then rapidly again towards the end of their life (Owen Connelan 1997: 215-225). Although more plausible as a general description, there is not a great deal of empirical evidence to support a particular curve for a particular building, which may place so much reliance on the opinion of an individual valuer that it renders the S-curve no more accurate than exponential or linear depreciation.

Both physical and functional obsolescence may reduce the value of the building to that of a disimprovement – a negative value equal at worst to the cost of demolition.

The profits method of valuation

The profits method (Valuation Office Agency vol 4 sect 6) is also known as the receipts and expenditure method, the income approach, the accounts method, the Treasury method and the residual method.

This method follows a rather different course depending on whether it can be assumed that the land is currently being put to the Highest and Best Use (HABU) – the use that will produce the highest return on investment that is physically possible, legally permissible, financially feasible and maximally productive. The surveyor has to make a judgement about what is the highest and best use in order to apply this method of valuation.

Receipts and expenditure method

If it can be assumed that the current use is the highest and best use, the surveyor analyses the business accounts and subtracts all costs (expenditure), including the notional cost of borrowing the capital invested in improvements but not the land, from the gross income (receipts). The difference is the market rent of the land.

If it cannot be assumed that the land is being put to its highest and best use, the only option is for the surveyor to conduct a thought experiment. They identify the highest and best use; estimate the hypothetical net income of the developed property from this use (which may simply be a more lucrative return for the current use following increased investment); estimate the cost of the necessary hypothetical improvements; subtract all costs, including the cost of borrowing the capital invested in the improvements; and then calculate a hypothetical market rent.

This thought experiment may be described as the residual method, particularly when it is used to assess the market value of development land. Here:

Residual site value = Gross Development Value – Total Development Cost – Developer's Profit

(The term 'residual approach' is also used to describe the cost approach (Frances Plimmer 1998 6.6.12).

The profits method is highly sensitive to the assumptions that are made about a large number of variables. But it does ensure that properties can be valued, even where there are no comparables, without having to expose them to the market. The profits method provides a way to estimate the value of land for which there are no available comparables by estimating what a tenant could afford to pay for it. It is unlikely to be put to use in a stewardship economy.

The Depreciated Replacement Cost of a building provides a reasonable estimate of what the building is worth to its owner, just as the Depreciated Replacement Cost provides a reasonable measure of what a caravan is worth. The idea of the Depreciated Replacement Cost of a building, and the experience that valuers have in estimating it, will prove invaluable when considering how best to value land in a stewardship economy.

As will be seen below (Chapter 7), in a stewardship economy the Depreciated Replacement Cost of buildings is never subtracted from the value of a whole property to arrive at a land value. Instead, they serve two other purposes: to ensure that the seller of a property receives a fair payment for those buildings, and to inform the buyer how much they will have to pay for these buildings before they make a bid for the stewardship fees they will offer for the land.

Chapter 5 Estimating the market rent of the UK

This chapter uses several approaches to make an approximate estimate of the market rent of the UK in 2009.

National accounts: the blue book

The United Kingdom National Accounts: the Blue Book (Office for National Statistics 2009) is the government's annual description of the national economy. It is based on the European System of National Accounts (ENA), which in turn is based on the United Nations System of National Accounts (SNA).

The Blue Book distinguishes between rent, which it defines as the property income from land and sub-soil resources; and rental, which is the income payable by the user of a fixed asset (artefact). The market rent of land in the UK should be easily identifiable from these accounts. The figures it allocates to rent are, however, extremely low because of the method used. Where the rental for buildings and rent for land is combined in a single payment, the Office for National Statistics allocates the whole amount to whichever is believed to be the larger. Agricultural rents and royalties for exploration for oil and gas account for most payments recorded as rent (Office for National Statistics 1998: 14.77). Payments for land used for business, commercial, industrial and housing are recorded as rental (Office for National Statistics 1998: 5.49) .

Agricultural rents

The total rent in the UK is given as £ 1.44 billion in 2008 (Office for National Statistics 2009:45), based on information from the Department for Rural Affairs. To obtain a realistic estimate of the market rent of agricultural land we would need to subtract the oil and gas royalties and reduce the figure by perhaps some 10 per cent to allow for the element of this 'rent' that is a return to improvements ('rental').

Commercial rents

The Blue Book allocates commercial rents to the category of rental, not rent. It does not seem to be possible to separate out the rent of the land used for business, commercial and industrial use from the figures in the Blue Book. According to the National Accounts, financial corporations are considered to pay no rent at all (Office for National Statistics 2009:154).

Housing rents

The final consumption expenditure of households for 2008 is given as £877 billion per year, of which £130 billion is accounted for as home rental payments (£38 billion as actual payments and £92 billion as imputed rental payments by owner-occupiers (Office for National Statistics 2009:232)). The imputed rental payments were benchmarked in 1991 and have been projected forwards. If these rental figures are reduced by a factor of 0.35 to remove the cost of the buildings, this gives a housing rent of around £45 billion per year.

Rent or market rent

The Blue Book figures are based on payments either being made or imputed at current values. The figures for rent are therefore underestimates of the market rent due to the current underuse and misallocation of land.

Total rent

All these figures seem surprisingly low. If we assume a yield of 5 per cent of market value on agricultural land the figures imply a market value of about £26 billion. With a UK agricultural area of around 17 million hectares this suggests that the average price of farmland should be about £600 per acre, which is an underestimate by at least a factor of five.

A yield of 5 per cent of market value on homes gives a total market value of about £2,600 billion for the homes of the UK (buildings plus land). With about £25.5 million households in the UK, this gives the average market price of a home as around

£100,000 – somewhat less when unoccupied and second homes are taken into account (c.f. actual average of £157,000).

In view of these results for agricultural and housing land, and the lack of information about commercial land values, an independent estimate of the current value of the land in the UK is required. It would be very helpful if the Office for National Statistics would prepare a set of satellite accounts in the Blue Book to account for land – just as they do, for example, with the environment.

Land value and GDP

The market rent of land rises with the level of economic activity, and it is generally presumed that a country's total market rent is broadly proportional to its GDP. Economists normally assume that the market rent of land amounts to somewhere between 2 per cent and 5 per cent of GDP (Ronald Banks: 1989:38).

The market rent of land is reduced by the taxes that a country levies (Stewardship Economy: Why?: Chapter 8). It is therefore likely to be a higher proportion of GDP in a relatively low-tax environment like the USA, and a lower proportion of GDP in a relatively high-tax environment like Denmark. The current market rent of the UK might therefore be expected to lie somewhere between the proportions of GDP that are found in the USA and Denmark.

Nicolaus Tideman has estimated the total market value of land in the USA in 2000 by subtracting the value of all capital (as estimated by the Department of Commerce) from the value of all household wealth (from data collected by the Federal Reserve Board) (Nicolaus Tideman 2004:15). The method is inevitably imprecise. It does not include the market rent of government land but, as Rana Roy (2004:18) has pointed out, it does include the value of the whole of the natural world (in particular oil) not just land.

This results in a total market value of $30.3 trillion from which he arrives at a market rent of $1.4 trillion (a yield of 4.7 per cent of market value), amounting to 12.8 per cent of GDP or $4600 per person (Nicolaus Tideman 2004:21). He suggests that this would be greater if a Land Value Tax was introduced as it would cause an increase in the efficiency of land use.

Morris Davis and Jonathan Heathcote (2004:11), using data from the Decennial Census of Housing, estimate that in 2003 the total market value of the land under existing residences in the USA was approximately equal to the GDP, equivalent to a value for market rent of around 5-8 per cent of GDP (assuming a yield of 5-8 per cent).

Denmark estimates the market rent of its land on a plot-by-plot basis for the purposes of Land Value Taxation. Here the total market rent of land was in the range of 5 to 10 per cent of GDP between 1965 and 1995 (John Muellbaur 2003:)

Using this approach, it seems reasonable to expect that the current market rent of the UK, as a proportion of GDP, lies between 5 per cent and 12.8 per cent – although this cannot be considered to be better than a guesstimate. With a UK GDP of £1,446 billion in 2008 this gives a range of £72 billion to £185 billion.

A spatial approach to valuing Great Britain

The market rents of most plots of land in the UK are not estimated, let alone publicly available. Estimates of the total market rent for the whole country can only be made at an aggregate level. Such an estimate is inevitably very approximate.

Updating Ronald Banks' estimate

In 1989 Ronald Banks (1989:39) and a group of colleagues set themselves the task of estimating the value of the land in Great Britain in 1985. One of the contributors used the same method to track the changes between 1985 and 1990, a time when land values were increasing rapidly (David Richards 1989:1).

Their core approach was a spatial method of assessment in which the value of each category of land is estimated by multiplying the area in this category by its average price per hectare.

They divided land use into broad categories of use: residential; industrial; commercial; agricultural and forests; and public services. They then subdivided each of these categories – for example, agricultural land according to the grade or use of land. For each sub-category and for each region of Great Britain they estimated the quantity of land as the number of hectares or dwellings; the average sale price of that category of land; and, by multiplication, the market value. This approach, though simple in principle, requires considerable professional judgement when reconciling data sets that have been collected by different agencies for different purposes at different times using different methods applied to different geographical boundaries.

Sale prices include both land and improvements. For each category of land use, they reduced the figures by an empirical factor, based on information from surveyors and valuers, to derive the value of the land from the value of the whole property (land + improvements). They used, for example, a factor of 0.9 for agricultural properties (where the land is the most valuable component of the property) and 0.35 for residential properties (where the building is the most valuable component). For comparison, in the USA the value of residential land (under 1-4 housing units) amounted to 46 per cent of the market value of the homes in 2003 compared with an average of 38 per cent over the preceding 30 years (Morris Davis and Jonathan Heathcote 2004:11).

See table on following page.

Where possible, the authors used more than one national data set, and identified both a market value for each category of land and a measure of the total area occupied by this category. These were used to produce the figures for market value in column 1.

		Britain		UK
		1985 Banks		Adjusted to 2009
	£bn	per cent	£bn	£bn
Category of land	**Market value**	**Yield**	**Market rent**	**Market rent**
Public service	64	5	3	20
Farm & woodland	48	5	2	15
Housing	249	8	20	121
Commerce	108	8	9	52
Industry	36	13	4	27
TOTAL excluding public land	**441**		**35**	**215**
Estimates of Market Rent 1985 and 2009				

Ronald Banks converted the market values to market rents (Column 3) by a factor that reflects the yield (Column 2) that land surveyors judged to be realistic for that category of use for that year (David Richards 1989:17 & Ronald Banks 1989:39). In the final column of the table, I have adjusted these market rents to January 2009 using the Department of Communities and Local Government (DCLG) index for house prices.

This approach gives an annual market rent of the privately held land of Great Britain in 2009 of £211 billion. For simplicity and comparison this excludes the market rent of government land (the government will be liable to pay stewardship fees for its land and so there will be no net revenue from this land).

Northern Ireland contributes just over 2 per cent of the UK's GDP, and if we assume that total land value is proportional to GDP the total should be uplifted to £215 billion to obtain the market rent for the whole of the United Kingdom.

The confidence limits for the estimates of area and value may be more than 10 per cent, so the confidence limits for the market rent may be more than 20 per cent - that is to say between £172 billion and £258 billion.

To provide a minimal cross-check I have estimated the total market rent of housing land in 2009 (using 2009 data from the Land Registry for the average price of a dwelling and 2007 data from the DCLG for the total number of dwellings). This gives a total for housing land of £116 billion. This is an underestimate for three reasons: the Land Registry data is a geometric mean which is always lower than the arithmetic mean: the DCLG figures are slightly behind the times; the figure does not include the value of any land designated for building but on which there are no dwellings. This £116 billion is not far off the figure of £121 billion in the table with a total market rent (excluding public land) of £215 billion calculated for 2009 from the Banks estimates.

A working hypothesis

I shall assume that the market rent of the UK is £180 billion in 2009. Although at 12.5 per cent of GDP this is somewhat higher than the percentage of GDP reported from Denmark, it is close to the lowest boundary of the value assessed by the spatial method. This is, I believe, a conservative estimate of the market rent of the UK. The amount of the actual stewardship fees that could be collected is influenced by several other factors.

Stewardship fees due ought to be higher than estimated as the land would be valued at its highest and best use, not its current use. In addition, rents would rise as the result of the boost to the economy caused by either the removal of orthodox taxes with their deadweight loss or by the distribution of a Universal Income. However, any increase in fees would be mitigated by the reduction in fees resulting from the pressure of a stewardship economy to bring empty homes, second homes and building plots on to the market, increasing supply of homes and reducing their market rent.

Part III How to value land in a stewardship economy

If the steward has to pay 100 per cent of the market rent of land as stewardship fees, the market rent of the land (net of stewardship fees) is zero. This assumes that stewardship fees are always equal to market rents, that is to say that revaluation is ongoing or at least frequent.

The market value is also zero, as the steward can anticipate no revenue from the land net of stewardship fees. This means that the land market used in ownership economies, whether for purchase or for rent, cannot be used to determine the market rent.

A stewardship economy needs a new sort of land market in which the market rent, and the stewardship fees, are established directly in the market. It needs to be able to establish the market rent of both unimproved land (Chapter 6) and improved land (Chapter 7).

Chapter 6   Unimproved land

This chapter explores how the market rent of land is established when a Land Value Tax is levied at increasing proportions of the market rent of land.

First it discusses the valuation of land in an ownership economy where some proportion of the market rent, but less than 100 per cent, is collected as a Land Value Tax. This is a situation in which there is an established approach that has been tried and tested in the many jurisdictions around the world that collect a proportion of market rent as a Land Value Tax, even though there is no experience of this in the UK.

It is clear, from this experience, that it is straightforward to estimate the market value of all land when Land Value Tax is levied at up to 50 per cent of market rent. The challenge of separating the value of buildings from the value of the land on which they are located (Chapter 7) can easily be met.

If this book was describing how to go about implementing Land Value Taxation at up to 50 per cent of market rent, there would be no need for an extended discussion of valuation. But as an established stewardship economy is one in which 100 per cent of the market rent of land is collected as stewardship fees, the implications for valuation and for the land market need to be considered.

This chapter therefore goes on to discuss the situation in a stewardship economy in which 100 per cent of the market rent is collected. It focuses on the simplest case, that of unimproved land – the next chapter discusses land with buildings and other improvements.

Land Value Tax in an ownership economy

The table below sets out a thought experiment, not a policy proposal. It shows what would happen to the market value of land when a Land Value Tax, paid by the landowner (not a tenant), is set at various levels between 0 per cent and 100 per cent of market rent. The example is a site for which a tenant would be prepared to pay the landowner a market rent of £5,000 per year. The calculations assume that the yield is 5 per cent (the market rent is 5 per cent of the market value) and that there are no changes in any other taxes.

	Market rent (gross annual) (A)	Land Value Tax as per cent of market rent (B)	Land Value Tax (annual) (C)	Market rent net of Land Value Tax (D)	Market value (net market rent / yield) (E)	Land Value Tax as per cent of market value (F)
[1]	£ 5,000	0 %	£ 0	£ 5,000	£ 100,000	0 %
[2]	£ 5,000	5 %	£ 250	£4,750	£ 95,000	0.3 %
[3]	£ 5,000	25 %	£1,250	£3,750	£75,000	1.7 %
[4]	£ 5,000	50 %	£ 2,500	£ 2,500	£ 50,000	5 %
[5]	£ 5,000	66 %	£ 3,333	£ 1,667	£ 33,333	10 %
[6]	£ 5,000	80 %	£ 4,000	£ 1,000	£ 20,000	20 %
[7]	£ 5,000	90 %	£ 4,500	£ 500	£ 10,000	45 %
[8]	£ 5,000	100 %	£ 5,000	£0	£0	infinite

Impact of LVT on market rent and market value

In an ownership economy with no Land Value Tax (row 1), the land has a market rent of £5,000 and market value of £100,000.

Introducing a Land Value Tax at 50 per cent of the gross market rent (row 4) halves the market rent net of Land Value Tax (column D) and so halves the market value (column E).

Working down the table, columns (D) and (E) show how the Land Value Tax erodes both the (net) market rent and the market value. Above 50 per cent the Land Value Tax becomes an increasingly important consideration for a purchaser, as shown in Column (F) and the market value less important.

Objections to Land Value Taxation

Erosion of the tax base

One of the objections that is frequently raised by orthodox economists is that Land Value Taxation 'erodes its own tax base'. This is a particularly bizarre objection as a Land Value Tax stimulates the economy, and so leads to a rise in the market rent of land.

The objection arises from a misunderstanding or misrepresentation of the nature of Land Value Tax – that the tax is levied on the market value, rather than on the (gross) market rent. Objectors point out, correctly, that if 100 per cent of the market rent is collected as tax then the rent received net of tax is zero – and so the market value of land (equal to the discounted stream of expected future revenue) is also zero (row [7]). The objection can be easily dismissed – the tax is based not on the market value of land, or on its net market rent, but on its gross market rent. Even if the market value is zero there is no erosion of the tax base.

Destruction of the land market

Taxation at 5 per cent of gross market rent (row 2) does not disturb the traditional land market at all, whether the tax is calculated as a percentage of net market rent or market value (column F).

As the percentage rises, the bidder for the land has to give increasing attention to the recurrent annual costs compared with the purchase price. Imagine acquiring land on which a Land Value Tax is levied at 50 per cent of (gross) market rent (row 3). If you want to rent, you will have to be aware that you will need to bid a market rent of £2,500 per year in order to pay a total (including Land Value Tax) of £5,000 per year. If you want to buy, the land will cost £50,000 and there will be an additional liability to pay a Land Value Tax of £2,500 per year. The annual cost has become as significant a factor as the purchase price.

If the Land Value Tax is levied at 90 per cent of gross market rent (row 6), the annual liability of £4,500 dwarfs the purchase price of £10,000. The purchaser will be thinking 'how much Land Value Tax can I afford to pay each year' and then calculating how much they need to offer as a purchase price.

There is therefore a limit to the proportion of market rent that can be captured as tax when the valuation is based on sales in the traditional land market. It's difficult to be sure what the limit is but it will be considerably less than 100 per cent of the market rent – even 50 per cent of the gross market rent (100 per cent of the net market rent) seems likely to be unachievable.

The level of taxation becomes exquisitely sensitive to errors in the market value of the property, and open to challenge. This problem is tacitly recognised by most supporters of Land Value Taxation who advocate gradual change from low rates of Land Value Taxation, and approach higher rates in the spirit of 'let's cross that bridge when we come to it'.

Collecting 100 per cent of the (gross) market rent as Land Value Tax is not a problem if the valuation is based on a direct observation of the market rent of the property. The land market would need to take a different form that invites offers of the market rent rather than, or as well as, the market value. To achieve a stewardship economy a new land market is needed.

Valuation for LVT

There is no shortage of examples from jurisdictions where Land Value Taxation is in place such as Denmark and the USA

(Chapter 2 & Ted Gwartney 1999);   and from feasibility studies in the UK such as the Whitstable valuations carried out by Hector Wilks for the Henry George Foundation in 1963 and 1973 (Hector Wilks 1964 & 1974). Here valuers have been able to use market transactions to establish land values in spite of a property tax being levied, albeit not at high rates.

Implications for the land market

Valuation by market transaction

In an ownership economy the value (i.e., sale price) or rent of land is established wherever there is an open market transaction, by and in that transaction itself. This provides a 'gold standard' for the market value if the offers are to purchase the land;   or for the market rent if the offers are to rent it.

The market rent of land may be established directly in this way; or derived from the market value using the investment approach or estimated by comparison with the market rent of comparable sites (Chapter 4).

Obtaining the maximum price

In an ownership economy, when an owner wants to dispose of a plot of land they handle the transaction themselves. With the exception of gifts and bequests the land is usually sold by private treaty. It is offered on the market at a price that reflects the owner's, or their estate agent's, judgement of its market value, and sold at a price that is negotiated around this figure, which is the highest that can be achieved.

Some properties in ownership economies are sold at auction – particularly when they need to be sold quickly or are difficult to value. This may be because the property is unique, because it needs substantial refurbishment or because times are uncertain, and an auction sale always delivers a price that cannot be challenged because an auction is clear and transparent.

Whether a property is sold by private treaty or by auction, the departing owner tries to get the best price for the land. This is very different from the situation in a stewardship economy, where the outgoing steward has no financial incentive to pass the land on to the person who would be prepared to pay the highest stewardship fees, as these will be paid to the community not to themselves. A stewardship economy needs a new land market in which transfers of property rights are conducted on behalf of the community not the outgoing steward.

On the island of Folegandros in the Cyclades, the church owns most of the agricultural land. The use-right to each plot is offered at auction, though unlike stewardship these auctions are held annually. Some plots receive no bids and remain uncultivated. Other plots, particularly those in the valleys where there is water, are allocated to the highest bidder.

This appears to be an efficient way of allocating the scarce resource of viable agricultural plots – whoever uses the land for the next year will be, more or less, the people who are confident they can make best use of it.

The church's landholding has been built up from bequests. The motivation for these bequests has been an altruistic concern for the long-term spiritual well-being of future generations on the island. The rent, determined at auction, is used for the benefit of the whole community – for maintaining the fabric of its churches and paying its priests. So, the auction also seems to have a sense of fairness – people who use a scarce natural resource are compensating the whole community.

One obvious problem is that this provides no incentive for the user of a plot to improve it – to build a dam, for example, or even deep trenching – as the payoff in one year would be insufficient to justify the investment of time and money. One way to overcome this would be for the church to invest some of its income in improvements, which it might do both to increase the economic well-being of its community and in the expectation that the investment could be recouped through higher income at subsequent auctions.

Stewardship economy

Imagine an established stewardship economy where 100 per cent of the market rent of all land is collected as stewardship fees. Suppose that a steward wants to vacate a plot of land which has no improvements at all on it, and several people want to acquire it. Who gets the land? To whom is it allocated? How is the market rent established? How does the land market work?

The net market rent, and the market price of the plot is zero, so it can't be bought and sold in a traditional land market. But it does command a gross market rent, and there is competition to become its steward. The land market needs to change from the present one in which a perpetual ownership right is bought and sold to one in which a use-right is allocated to whoever commits to paying the market rent. This requires a New Land Market, supervised by the Land Stewardship Trust.

The New Land Market

The direct 'deal' between buyer and seller, mediated in various ways by estate agents, that characterises ownership economies would provide the seller in a stewardship economy with no financial incentive to ensure that that the new steward is the person who values the land most and is prepared to pay the highest stewardship fees.

In the New Land Market all properties are transferred by auction, a transparent market transaction that determines the stewardship fees at the same instant as the (gross) market rent.

Bidders in the New Land Market will be aware of any planning restrictions, and the bids made will naturally be based not on the current use of the land but on its 'Highest and Best Use' (HABU) – the use that is anticipated to produce the greatest net earnings and which is physically possible, legally permissible and financially feasible.

The auction directly establishes the (gross) annual market rent of the site, the stewardship fees and the new steward all in the same transaction. There is no erosion of the tax base, and the land market has been transformed, not destroyed. The New Land

Market, with minor refinements, is capable of handling land with improvements (Chapter 7) and supporting any form of transition to stewardship (Chapter 11). There are many possible auction methods (Chapter 8) . A web-based platform, similar to eBay, would probably be most appropriate.

This new property market might at first sight seem to be undue state involvement in the private matter of a property transfer. But all market transactions already take place within a context that is determined and regulated by the state. This context includes a law of contract, enforceable property rights and a mechanism for the transfer of these rights.

Once the successful bidder has acquired the use of the land, they will need to pay stewardship fees that are regularly updated.

Keeping the valuation register up to date

One of the major failings of existing property taxes, including Council Tax and National Non-Domestic (Business) Rates, has been the infrequent revaluations. One cause has been the political unpopularity of revaluation, another has been the work involved in visiting each property to establish its new value. Such visits are no longer necessary as Computer Assisted Mass Appraisal (Chapter 3) develops a database of property transactions that is updated as they occur. This has the potential to update the entry for a property in the valuation register on a rolling basis each time that the sale of a comparable property is recorded, even though tax liabilities would only be updated annually.

Annual revaluations

The Land Stewardship Trust needs to produce regular (at least annual) estimates of the market rent of all properties, taking in to account its knowledge of transactions for comparable sites on the open market in the recent past.

Choice of comparables

For each site the Land Stewardship Trust would need to select a number of designated comparable sites. The list of comparables would ideally be selected before they came to market and the steward would be encouraged to review this list, challenge any of the comparables and suggest alternatives that would be more nearly comparable.

The challenge of finding enough undeveloped sites, with no improvements, would be great and it is unlikely that undeveloped land in high- consumption economies can in practice be valued by comparison with other undeveloped sites.

Revaluation by direct comparison

One way of using comparables in a stewardship economy would be the obvious approach of direct comparison. Each year the market rent of the site to be valued, the index site, would be determined directly by comparison with the stewardship fees of a bundle of comparables that had been transferred in the new land market during the previous year.

The advantage of this approach is that the market rent of the index site is established fairly and transparently – it is equal to the stewardship fees of a perfect comparable. The disadvantage is that it is dependent on finding comparables that are truly comparable – a difficult task (Chapter 3).

Revaluation by proportional comparison

An alternative to valuation by direct comparison is to use comparables not to establish a value directly but to establish the percentage by which the index property is judged to have changed in value over the previous year.

The advantage of this approach is that each year's valuation can be anchored in a genuine open market transaction for the index property itself at some time in the past. This means that, even if the comparables are 'similar' rather than 'the same', any inaccuracy will be applied only to the change in value since the last open market transaction, not to the total amount. This is the approach taken by automated valuation models.

The disadvantage is that the inaccuracies are likely to be cumulative, and over the years the valuation will drift away from the market value that would be revealed at auction. This reinforces the need for an appeal mechanism that allows the market value to be established directly in the market.

Appeal to the market

Since a valuer can give only an opinion of the market rent of a site by reference to comparables, stewardship requires an appeal mechanism. Since the estimate of the market rent is an opinion about the highest stewardship fees that would be bid if the land was exposed to the market, the most appropriate appeal mechanism is to do just that – to put the (unimproved) land on the market. This would provide a mechanism for handling:

- Disputes about the market rent. Appeal to the market would provide a mechanism for correcting any errors in revaluation, whether this is carried out by direct comparison or by proportional comparison.

- Lack of adequate comparables. Where a site has not been exposed to the market and there are genuinely no comparables – for example an airport, or a harbour – it may be necessary to assess its value using the receipts and expenditure approach (Chapter 4). If this proves contentious the alternative is to require that it be exposed to the market at periodic intervals. Sites like these are likely to provide the basis for a local monopoly, and periodic exposure to the market may be a good way of moderating this monopoly power.

- Falling land prices. Stewards could appeal in this way to reduce the level of their stewardship fees rapidly in situations where land values fall, either nationally during an economic downturn or locally due to deterioration in the local environment and circumstances.

Ransom sites

One challenge to valuation in an ownership economy may occur when a developer is trying to put together a large development across land owned by a number of different people. Sometimes one person who owns a small site that needs to be included may block a whole development. Here the owner might agree a higher selling price, a 'ransom', with the developer. Once the developer has bought it, does it any longer have a higher value than the surrounding sites? Does that question mean anything – is it only possible to talk about the value of the whole development site? And if the owner of the ransom site does not sell, what is its value?

This certainly falls outside the definition of 'market value'. Fortunately, the dilemma does not arise in a stewardship economy where the steward of the ransom site would receive only the assessed value of their improvements. If that was not enough to stimulate a transfer to the developer, the Land Stewardship Trust would select, as comparables, other similar sites in this or other developments with similar planning permissions. The current steward would then face paying higher stewardship fees, not an opportunity to secure a ransom. If they wanted to appeal against the valuation they could do so in the usual way.

Consequences of errors in valuation

Errors in valuation would, of course, cause problems for stewards and for the economy. That is why the valuations in a stewardship economy are based, as far as possible, on market transactions.

If the market rent is overestimated, potential stewards will not be willing to pay the stewardship fees for the land as they know that this exceeds the benefit they are likely to get from it. In this situation the land would remain unused, and the Land Stewardship Trust would need to put it on the market.

If the market rent is underestimated, the steward of the land will retain part for their own benefit, removing the incentive for the land to be used in the most economically efficient way. The Land Stewardship Trust would be alerted by evidence of stewards trying to sell their land. Underestimating the market rent also reduces the revenue available from stewardship fees.

This chapter has considered how a stewardship economy requires a New Land Market. Property transactions take place through a Land Stewardship Trust which allocates unimproved land to whoever bids the highest stewardship fees at auction. Valuations need to be kept up to date, for example by making annual adjustments based on comparisons with market transactions for comparable sites. This is supplemented by an appeal mechanism that enables a steward to expose their property to the market and obtain a valuation by market transaction.

Chapter 7   Improved land

This chapter explores how improved land would be valued using the New Land Market.

The major challenge, as in an ownership economy, is that there are generally few unimproved sites available as genuine comparables. One solution is an extension of the New Land Market (Chapter 6) in which improvements are valued by a surveyor, then willingness to pay the value of these improvements to the outgoing steward is a precondition for bidding for the land and this transaction determines the market rent of land, and so the stewardship fees.

This chapter describes this extension of the New Land Market, and some issues raised by the process. If the value of improved land is established at the time when it is transferred from one steward to another, the value of other plots of land (improved as well as unimproved) can be valued by comparison and this comparison automated using Computer Assisted Mass Appraisal (Chapter 3).

Comparison

Comparison with unimproved land
It would be possible to value improved land by comparison provided that there were enough comparable sites changing hands that were completely undeveloped. This is rarely possible in a high-consumption economy, even for agricultural land as this generally incorporates some improvements to which the steward can lay claim.

Comparison with improved land

About 5 per cent of developed properties in England and Wales change hands each year, so a few hundred designated comparables would provide a good chance that several were sold on the open market each year.

Mason Gaffney (1999: 23), drawing on his experience as Assessment Commissioner for the Canadian province of British Colombia, advocates annual revaluations and believes that this would be possible for 1,000,000 sites based on a careful analysis of a sample of 12,000 sites.

The aim of valuation in a stewardship economy

When a steward sells their property they receive a payment for the improvements, which they own, but the market value of the land will be zero. Potential stewards will compete for the stewardship of the property not by offering the highest purchase price for the whole property, as in an ownership economy, but by offering the highest market rent for the land alone, which will be paid as stewardship fees.

The aim of valuation in a stewardship economy is to ensure that the owner of a building or other improvements pays or receives a fair price when they buy or sell a property. The value needs to reflect the value of the building, including any additions made by the outgoing steward, with a realistic allowance for depreciation – just as depreciation is reflected in the price of second-hand cars or caravans.

When a property is sold in an ownership economy it is usually unclear whether any increase in its value is due to an increase in the value of the improvements, as many owners assume, or in the value of the land. It may be helpful to consider the case of a caravan which can be built, bought and sold independently of the land on which it may be located.

When a new caravan is sold, its price will be determined by supply and demand. If a manufacturer can manufacture a caravan for less than this price, it will make a profit. But in a competitive market, if this profit is large other manufacturers will increase the supply and bring down the price till it is close to the cost of manufacture. The value of manufactured goods, in a competitive market without monopolies, tends towards the cost of their manufacture.

When a building is constructed the cost to the developer is equal to the sum of the price of the land and the construction cost of the buildings (including all fees, cost of capital and normal levels of profit). If it is then sold on the open market for more than the cost to the developer, and there is similar land with similar planning conditions available to other builders, competition would then bring the sale price (market value) down to the cost to the developer – the cost of its manufacture. This is rarely possible, as no other builder can acquire that same building plot, and even imperfectly comparable plots are hard to come by. If the selling price remains higher than the cost to the developer it must be because the land is worth more than the developer paid for it, not because the building is worth more than it cost to construct it.

The appropriate approach to valuation, therefore, is for the price of the improvement to be settled first at a fair value, equal to the Depreciated Replacement Cost. Once this is settled, the market value of the land can be determined in the open market, in much the same way as in the case of unimproved land (Chapter 5).

New Land Market

The need for a new land market

A single market transaction for a property comprising land and buildings will always fail to distinguish between the component of its value contributed by the land and the component contributed by the improvements.

his means that there is a choice. One possibility, currently used to determine property values for the purposes of taxation, is for a valuer to assess the value of the land and for the market to determine the value of the buildings. There are well established ways of determining the value of a building that are independent of the location and value of its site, based on knowledge of construction costs. The main argument in favour of this approach is that modern Computer Assisted Mass Appraisal methods, drawing on knowledge of large numbers of pieces of information about each property, are capable of accurate and non-intrusive valuations of plots of land. The main argument against this approach is that it is necessarily derived either by comparison with unimproved land or by comparison with whole properties from which the value of the improvements have been subtracted.

The other possibility, described here as the New Land Market, is to put a value on the buildings and then use the market to determine the value of the land. The only certain way of determining the value of land is to see how much someone is prepared to pay for it. The main argument in favour of this approach is that it is easier to value buildings than land and that the value of the land is in each case genuinely established in the market. The main argument against it is that the ease of valuing buildings is an illusion, and that there are more appeals against building values than land values.

A fair value for improvements

So, in a stewardship economy we need a method of valuation that first establishes the capital value of improvements (which are owned, in the traditional sense, by the steward); then uses market mechanisms to determine the market rent of the land (which is collected as the stewardship fees). Chapter 6 has already described a New Land Market for the transfer of unimproved land which, with a few modifications, it is capable of putting a value on improved land:

- The Land Stewardship Trust determines a fair value for the improvements on each site, equal to the Depreciated Replacement Cost (Chapter 4).

- Property transfers take place through an auction conducted by the Land Stewardship Trust using the New Land Market (Chapter 6).

- A bidder is admitted to the auction only on the undertaking that, when they win the auction, they will pay the Depreciated Replacement Cost to the existing steward.

- The highest bid for the stewardship fees determines who the new steward will be and the stewardship fees they will pay.

- If there are no positive bids then the Depreciated Replacement Cost has been set too high. It is, after all, an estimate made by a valuer not even a market price.

- To establish a fair price for the improvements using market mechanisms the stewardship fees are set to zero and the improvements are auctioned to the highest bidder. This fair price is recorded, as an additional column in the Land Register, as the Registered Improvement Value.

- Registered Improvement Values that have not been re-valued in this way are assumed to be equal to the Depreciated Replacement Cost.

- If there are no bids for the improvements, the Registered Improvement Value is set to zero and negative bids (stewardship Support fees i.e., subsidies) are invited for the stewardship fees.

- The Land Stewardship Trust conducts annual revaluations of the stewardship fees for all properties using Computer Assisted Mass Appraisal. This revaluation is based on comparables that have been recently exposed to the market, perhaps by proportional comparison (Chapter 6) on the grounds that it has greater face validity in the short and medium term than direct comparison.

- At the time when the stewardship of a property is transferred, and at times when significant building work has been carried out, the improvement value is reassessed.

This method of valuation uses the same principles and practice as the Depreciated Replacement Cost approach in ownership economies Chapter 4), though it is applied to the buildings alone. The purpose of the valuation, like the purpose of this approach in an ownership economy, is to establish a fair value that represents what the property is really worth to the existing steward. There is no market for the buildings independently of the land, so the Depreciated Replacement Cost is the best available way to estimate Fair Value.

The approach differs, however, in the way that the Depreciated Replacement Cost is used. This value for the improvements is available to bidders before the auction of the whole property is conducted. The value of the land in isolation, then, is established in a market transaction in which the value is determined by the steward who intends to put the site to use. The role of the valuer is important in determining the Depreciated Replacement Cost, and in regularly updating land valuations by comparison, but they have no direct hand in setting the stewardship fees .

Where there are no recent market transactions for the site and no comparables, as in the case of airports, the receipts and expenditure method of valuation could be applied instead, but it is unlikely to be sufficiently robust in view of the numerous uncertainties. The best option here might be to assess the Depreciated Replacement Cost and require that the property be exposed to the market from time to time in the same sort of way that the franchises for train operating companies are currently put back out to tender.

Depreciation

The challenge for this new land market is that the surveyor's judgement of the Depreciated Replacement Cost (DRC) of a building will influence the stewardship fees that are bid for the property, not just the book value of a business as in an ownership economy. In a stewardship economy the Depreciated Replacement Cost (DRC) is being asked to carry the whole tax system.

Quantity surveyors have extensive professional experience of estimating the replacement cost and they should be in reasonable agreement about most buildings. The process represents an informed judgement based on a knowledge of recent tender prices for buildings of a similar construction (Chapter 4). This is the same approach as is taken when estimating the replacement cost of a building for insurance purposes.

The depreciation factor is likely to be much more contentious, as it does not correspond to any obvious market transaction. Identifying the right depreciation factor for any improvement is critically important if stewardship is to be fair and efficient.

Fairness

For an outgoing steward it is critically important to be fairly compensated for the improvement they own and may have built themselves. The Registered Improvement Value should represent the reality of the way that buildings deteriorate in value as closely as possible.

For an incoming steward the Registered Improvement Value of a property is, perhaps surprisingly, not of great importance. If the improvements are undervalued, for example by the application of an excessive depreciation factor, the new steward who benefits from buying the improvements cheaply will have to bid higher stewardship fees to secure the property. If the improvements are overvalued, for example if the depreciation factor is too low, the steward will not need to make such a high bid for the stewardship fees . What they gain by paying lower stewardship fees they lose by paying more for the improvements.

For the rest of us, the depreciation factor needs to be high enough to keep the Registered Improvement Value realistically low so that we all benefit from the payment of stewardship fees that really reflect the market rent of the unimproved land.

Efficiency

The depreciation factor should be low enough, and so the Depreciated Replacement Cost high enough, to ensure that:

- the Registered Improvement Value allows the steward to recoup their investment when they sell the property.

- construction is not penalised

- repair and improvement are encouraged, thereby increasing the longevity of buildings.

The depreciation factor should be high enough, and the Depreciated Replacement Cost low enough, to ensure that stewardship fees for that site will be realistically high and if a building ought to be replaced, demolition will not be discouraged by the high price paid for the improvements.

Most, but not all, buildings, like most cars or computers, have a limited life. At the end of this time there should be no financial incentive to keep using the building rather than replace it with a new one. If the depreciation factor is too low the Depreciated Replacement Cost will be so high that it discourages demolition and prolongs obsolescent use.

One way to assess a depreciation factor would be for a surveyor to make a judgement on a building-by-building basis, taking account of the costs of refurbishment to as-new condition, higher maintenance costs of old buildings and so on as described for an ownership economy (Chapter 4). The problem with this sort of approach is that the opinion of a surveyor may seem arbitrary to the steward, particularly at a time when they are selling the property or exposing it to the market as an appeal against revaluation. It is difficult for anyone who has lived in an ownership economy to accept the idea that the value of a house falls over time like that of a car or a caravan. The assessment of a depreciation factor by a surveyor would itself require an appeals procedure that would have plenty of work to do.

Adjustments would need to be made later if the building's condition is clearly worse than anticipated, or if it was judged to have a much longer life expectancy. The Land Stewardship Trust's surveyor would have to exercise an element of judgement.

What really matters is that the depreciation factor should be:

- Low enough to provide a fair price for an owner who is selling their property

- High enough that the price of the improvements does not deter appropriate redevelopment

- Certain enough not to lead to many appeals.

To meet these needs there is a lot to be said for the Land Stewardship Trust to declare a range of rates of depreciation that are applied in a standard way. The trajectory of depreciation needs to mirror the expected rate of economic and functional obsolescence, reflecting the anticipated life of the building. It needs to be tailored to the type and quality of construction and should ideally be agreed and in place at the time when the building is designed and built.

How much to depreciate?

Buildings need regular maintenance. If the cost of outstanding maintenance work on a building in a stewardship economy were to be greater than its Registered Improvement Value, the steward would have no financial incentive to carry out further maintenance as this expenditure would not be recouped when the property was sold.

This might lead stewards to neglect their buildings and other improvements, leading to a downward spiral and ultimately demolition. It's unlikely that any planning regulations would adequately counter this, so it seems sensible to ensure that the value of a well-maintained improvement does not fall too low until it requires demolition.

Stewart Brand (1994:112) identifies a rule of thumb about abandonment of buildings in an ownership economy. If the repairs will cost more than half the value of the building, it will be demolished rather than repaired. This suggests that the improvement value, if it were to be assessed assuming a standard trajectory of depreciation, should probably not fall below 50 per cent of the replacement cost while the buildings are judged to be worthy of preservation.

How fast to depreciate?

There are some clues about the appropriate rate of depreciation from ownership economies. These arise from our experience of agricultural improvements, the longevity of buildings, the value of leasehold interests and the rate of depreciation that is used for tax purposes.

Agricultural improvements

There are many ways in which farmers may improve the productivity of their land. Some of these, like sprinkler irrigation and the application of inorganic fertilisers or pesticides, have a short time scale and the expenditure is an input cost to the business rather than an improvement. Other developments have longer-term consequences – drainage, terracing, increased biomass in the soil, small dams and watercourses for example. If a steward is to have a financial incentive to make these changes, these developments should be treated as improvements so the investment can be at least partially recouped when they sell the property. In time, however, the improvements merge with the land and become part of it.

There is a lot of experience of handling the depreciation of agricultural improvements in an ownership economy because tenants frequently make improvements, and disimprovements, to their landlord's property. These need to be handled fairly at the end of a tenancy in just the same way as any goods (livestock and deadstock), the current season's crops and fertiliser applied, and the value of the unexhausted lime applied. For how long can the tenant reasonably lay claim to an improvement they make, and when should it be considered to have 'merged' with the land?

The practice in ownership economies reflects a widespread acceptance that a person's claim to the value of the improvements is limited in time. Tenants' improvements are subject to a write-off period, after which the full value of the improvement belongs to the landlord. This period is frequently agreed at the outset, when the landlord grants consent for the improvement.

If a landlord grants open unrestricted consent, with no specified write-off period, the Agricultural Holdings Act (1986: Section 66) requires that the compensation at the end of a tenancy should be equal to the amount by which that improvement increases the value of the holding. This is normally calculated by estimating the rental value of the holding (land plus improvements) with and without the improvement in question. This rental value is then capitalised at an appropriate rate of interest over its expected lifetime. Valuers are thus familiar with assessing the expected life of improvements. Examples in a guide to agricultural valuers (R Gwyn Williams 2008:46) include 15 years for electrical wiring, 50 years for a Dutch Barn, 30 years for a covered cattle yard and 20 years for land drainage. Ten or even fifteen years is too short for most developments, though the building of specialised developments like pig and dairy units may not be deterred by such short write-off periods.

In a stewardship economy, too, improvements should be depreciated over a period that more or less equals the expected life of the improvement.

The longevity of buildings

Some buildings, for example those with timber frame or stone construction, last for hundreds and sometimes even thousands of years. Buildings of conventional construction last decades.

As commercial buildings age, their market rent per square foot falls behind that of more recently constructed buildings. Property investors estimate that commercial buildings will require a refurbishment costing at least 30 per cent of its replacement cost somewhere between every 11 years (shopping centres) and every 25 years (warehouses) (Roger Flanagan et al 1989:44). On average, a commercial building's market value and market rent halves by the time it is 20 years old (Stewart Brand 1994/1995:112).

The decision whether to refurbish or replace usually comes in the crucial second thirty years of its life when the building is out of fashion, in poor repair and most vulnerable to demolition (Stewart Brand 1994:100).

The value of leasehold interests

Another clue to how fast to depreciate improvements is the rate at which the value of a property falls towards the end of a long lease in an ownership economy. A property with a lease of 100 years has almost the same value as a freehold property, and it is only when the lease falls below 70-80 years that its value begins to fall significantly.   This suggests that a building in a stewardship economy could be depreciated over 70-80 years without discouraging its construction and purchase.

Depreciation for tax purposes

Another clue to the appropriate rate of depreciation comes from the length of time over which investments can currently be written off for tax purposes. Governments generally tend to use their tax regimes to encourage investment by business. When the UK government wanted to encourage investment in information technology, it reduced the depreciation period so that computers could be depreciated for tax purposes by 100 per cent in their year of purchase. In the USA, commercial buildings are depreciated over 31½ years and residential buildings over 27½ years. Assuming that the government is doing what it can to stimulate business, the true length of time over which buildings depreciate is likely to be greater than 27½ years.

The rates of depreciation as well as the length of time for depreciation give another insight. The depreciation rates for buildings used by tax authorities in ownership economies are in the region of 2.5-4.0 per cent (Fred Harrison 2005:266).

Australia	2.5 per cent	over 40 years
USA	3.64 per cent	over 27.5 years
Canada	4 per cent	declining

 There are many advantages to selecting a simple standard trajectory for depreciation, for example exponential;   and a standard rate of depreciation on all buildings in the first instance. If an annual depreciation rate is set at 2 per cent, this would reduce the improvement value to half after 35 years (0.98^{35}). With an inflation rate of 3 per cent in the replacement cost, the Depreciated Replacement Cost would increase over 40 per cent (1.01^{35}) in nominal (money) terms. This could be politically acceptable as well as approximating to the way buildings really do deteriorate – and no doubt these suggested figures could be improved.

Instead of choosing 2 per cent as a depreciation factor it might be better to set it at half the rate of inflation. One reason is that it then delivers an increase in the nominal value of the Depreciated Replacement Cost no matter what the rate of inflation might be. Another reason is that this is equivalent to fully depreciating the value of the building but not depreciating the value of the land (assuming that the value of the property is about half attributed to the land and half to the building).

There may be a good case for the depreciation rate to be negotiable within a range at the time of construction, depending on the anticipated lifespan of the building as judged by the quality of construction.

An additional 'disimprovement value' would be added at any time by a surveyor if a greater rate of physical deterioration, or of functional obsolescence, was observed when compared with that anticipated. This disimprovement value would be subtracted from the improvement value, though this would be reversed if the building were repaired or restored.

Whatever the rate of depreciation, the Depreciated Replacement Cost should not fall below 50 per cent of the replacement cost if the building is worth preserving, in order to maintain a financial incentive to repair it. This rule of thumb applies to listed buildings and indeed to any building, at any stage in its life, that it would make sense to preserve rather than demolish. Once the Land Stewardship Trust judges that it would best be demolished the Depreciated Replacement Cost should fall to zero.

Agricultural improvements might be depreciated more rapidly than other buildings, using write-off periods that are similar to those in ownership economies.

Could this lead to over-development?

Suppose a developer invests the same amount in a new building in a stewardship economy as they would have done in an ownership economy. Provided it is a well conceived investment, the developed site will generate the level of income needed not just to pay for the improvements but also to pay the stewardship Fees .

But in a stewardship economy the stewardship Fees are not a 'given' cost. If the developer invests more in the development, the Registered Improvement Value will be higher and so the stewardship fees will be lower. By increasing the level of development beyond what would be financially prudent – imagine a gold-plated building – the developer might try to 'game' the tax system to reduce the stewardship fees , perhaps even to zero.

There would, however, be no financial incentive to overdevelop the site in this way unless the development genuinely made the business more profitable. Assuming that the developer borrows a capital sum to fund the overdevelopment, the reduction in the stewardship fees would be broadly equal to the interest payable on this loan. If the developer funds the overdevelopment directly, the reduction in stewardship fees would be broadly equal to the opportunity cost of the investment.

At the time of sale, the increased improvement value would be offset by the outstanding loan for the capital that was used for the overdevelopment. Even a small rate of depreciation of the improvements would render this an unprofitable strategy.

If this financial logic proved to be insufficient to deter overdevelopment, there is a further approach that is available to prevent it. The replacement cost is depreciated by both structural and functional obsolescence, and in a clearly overspecified building the valuer will recognise the degree of functional obsolescence at the outset, reducing the Depreciated Replacement Cost.

Stewardship fees and 'land value'

If a site was seriously overdeveloped the stewardship fees could fall to zero, though this is unlikely to happen. This might suggest that the method proposed for establishing the stewardship fees is flawed and that what is needed after all is an assessment method that values the site by comparison with a genuinely unimproved site.

118

This is not a fundamental problem. Rather it is like the situation in an ownership economy where the value of a developed site, on which there is an obsolescent building, is less than the value of the same site once the building has been demolished and the site cleared.

It does mean, however, that any comparable site must be encumbered with a similar building (as well as having other shared attributes such as similar planning restrictions).

Preservation of buildings

The advantages of preservation

Although a small number of old cars are highly desirable, most people find a new car more desirable than an old car of the same specification. This is probably true for the majority of offices, shops and industrial plant. For other sorts of building, particularly homes, old buildings may be desirable for aesthetic reasons, though this is likely to be increasingly outweighed by the low running costs of well insulated modern buildings.

Stewart Brand describes two sorts of buildings that last a long time. One he describes as the High Road, elegant and well-built structures that come to be recognised as beautiful even if that is not how they were originally seen. The other is the Low Road, structures that are responsive to the needs of their occupants and can be re-used and re-fashioned for a series of uses (Stewart Brand 1994: 91).

As he points out, the reasons to preserve old buildings are not limited to the aesthetic. The advantages of preservation over demolition and new building include:

- cost-effectiveness – it is usually cheaper, quicker and less disruptive

- environmental benefits – it generally uses less materials and less energy

- urban regeneration – it leads to mixed neighbourhoods, whose benefits have been so eloquently described by Jane

Jacobs (1961/1992), and small-scale change allows long-term continuity of occupation

- tourism – visitors are attracted to historic buildings.

A 'High Road' building may survive into the very long term simply because it is treasured, and therefore well maintained. There may no longer be a king or courtiers to use a palace, but it survives as a museum, for example. It is this adaptability that is the key to survival of most buildings, particularly those on the Low Road. If a building is flexible in its division of space and its provision of services, it will attract further investment to reshape and refit it so that it remains useful. Some buildings may be easily adapted, and Stewart Brand gives the example of 19th century factories, constructed soundly with floors capable of carrying machinery, that live on as offices, studios, workshops and homes. But an office block that has no other function and cannot adapt to new uses, or even styles of work, is unlikely to survive.

Stewardship and preservation of buildings

There are at least three ways in which stewardship is more likely than ownership to foster the preservation of buildings.

Stewart Brand (1994: 81-82) points out that buildings survive slow and gentle economic cycles – on the upswing people rehabilitate marginal structures, on the downswing they stay put and repair. But in times of rapid upswing the value of land rises so much that it stimulates greater levels of development, so that even quite new buildings are torn down – in the real estate boom in Tokyo in the 1980s, high-rises were being torn down after only 5 years and the average life of a building in Tokyo was 17 years. And when the downswing is severe there is less rent, less maintenance, and more buildings deteriorate to the point where they need to be demolished. Economic cycles are likely to be less extreme in a stewardship economy, which would reduce the neglect and premature demolition of buildings.

High quality construction, energy efficiency, and ease of maintenance all make it more likely that the building will survive. A well designed and constructed building will attract a lower rate of depreciation, be valued more highly and so reduce the fees that a steward would pay for the land on which it is sited. This should encourage the person who commissions a new building to invest in features that will pay off as lower stewardship fees in the long run.

In ownership economies some property taxes actually encourage the premature destruction of buildings (Chapter 2). stewardship fees do not have this effect as they are not related to current use or the extent of the improvements – provided that the Depreciated Replacement Cost of improvements is correctly assessed.

Improvements incorporated into the land

The fundamental proposition of Stewardship Economy: Private Property without Private Ownership is that land and improvements are distinct categories that require different sorts of property rights. And the purpose of this whole chapter is to propose a way to arrive at separate valuations of the market rent of a site and of the capital value of the buildings on that site. But before going any further I'm going to qualify this 'black and white' distinction between land and improvements by suggesting that, over time, improvements can be considered to merge with, and become part of, the natural world.

The landscape in almost all parts of the world, from the Sahara desert to the Scottish highlands, has been shaped through interaction between people and the natural world. What makes land and the natural world different from other things that are fixed in supply is not that they are 'untouched by human hand', but that in most cases no individual can reasonably lay claim to the value of the changes that have been brought about. Changes that are initially individually owned become our collective inheritance and, over time, can be considered to become part of the 'natural' world. At this point the improvement has depreciated by 100%. Agricultural improvements were discussed above; suggested arrangements for buildings and trees follow.

Buildings

In the same way as in an ownership economy, functional buildings are owned by their steward. Buildings that have fallen out of use and are ruined or demolished should probably be considered to have returned to nature and no longer treated as improvements that can be owned.

Trees

Crops, particularly those with a long life like trees, can provide a difficult challenge in making an appropriate distinction between land and improvements. The important distinction is not between the living and the non-living but, as with agricultural improvements, between things the steward can claim to own and things that they cannot.

Where trees occur wild in nature, or when they are very old, they should be treated as 'land' rather than 'improvements'. Even if they were planted by an identifiable individual they are part of our shared inheritance of the natural world.

The consequence of this classification is that the market rent of the land increases as the value of the trees increases. It falls when the trees are harvested. The owner would then be deemed to have inflicted a 'disimprovement' on the land and would have to make a payment equal to the discounted sum of lost stewardship fees. This would discourage the felling of historic and environmentally important trees. If a tree dies naturally, the steward needs to be able to discharge their duty by replanting.

Trees can, by contrast, be grown as a cash crop. In a stewardship economy, crops are designated and valued as improvements. The stewardship fees, which reflect the market rent of the unimproved land, then remain constant throughout the growing cycle. The steward can harvest and sell the crop when they wish, without any disincentive, as they own it in the conventional way. For instrumental rather than principled reasons these crops are not classified as part of the natural world.

There are numerous ways in which a stewardship economy could distinguish between trees and other crops that are 'land' and those that are 'improvements'. One is to invite an owner to register newly planted trees as 'improvements'. By charging a fee for each application, rather than paying for each tree, only commercial tree growers would seek this designation. Existing plantations could also be registered as improvements rather than as land, provided that they are managed in a sustainable way. Woodland, and trees planted for non-commercial reasons, would be treated as land not as an improvement.

Leasehold and multiple ownership

A fundamental requirement of stewardship is the establishment of a comprehensive land register, including leasehold interests.

Improved land, even more than unimproved land, may be subject to a variety of property rights. Property rights are complex and even in a stewardship economy, while there will be one overall steward of each site (the equivalent of the freeholder in an ownership economy), there may be any number of long-term, medium-term and short-term leaseholders as well as a variety of under-leases, sub-leases, shortholds and licences. There may be other rights such as mortgages, rights of way, clawback agreements, leasehold reform rights, rights of pre-emption, easements and so on.

It is the responsibility of all those who have an interest in a property to ensure that this interest is registered with the Land Registry. Whereas land taxes in ownership economies fall on the occupier, in a stewardship economy the stewardship fees fall on everyone who has an interest in the property and so who benefits from a share of the market rent (including notional rent) of the site. These interests include not just those of the overall steward but also the various leaseholders and possibly some of the holders of licences, easements and leasehold reform rights. They probably should not include shorthold tenancies that cannot be re-assigned. In an established stewardship economy, the market value of land is zero and so there are no mortgage interests in land.

The various stewardship fees add up to the total stewardship fees for the site – any marriage value (Chapter 3) is ignored.

The steps to be taken when allocating the improvement values and stewardship fees, for example for a block of flats, are:

- First, establish the total improvement value for all the improvements on the whole site. For new buildings this is the construction cost, for older buildings the Depreciated Replacement Cost.

- Allocate the improvement value amongst the various interests. This is difficult but follows the principles familiar in ownership economies and exercised in leasehold enfranchisement.

- Use these improvement values at the auctions when the various interests are next transferred.

- Depreciate these improvement values at the same rate as the whole building.

During transition to stewardship, any one of the parties can appeal if they feel that the Land Stewardship Trust has undervalued its interest. In this case:

- All the interests are exposed to the market, using the pre-appeal improvement values, and stewardship fees are established.

- The pre-appeal improvement values are then adjusted amongst the interests in proportion to the stewardship fees established in the market.

- Once these improvement values have been decided, they becomes the baseline for annual depreciation or assessed depreciation.

The costs and inconvenience of handling sites with multiple ownership should not be underestimated. It may be expected that some levels of leaseholder will choose to sell their interest to a higher or lower level steward. The experience of leasehold enfranchisement in ownership economies, which has of course been driven by legislation, has led to simplification of landholdings and very often resulted in just two levels of ownership – the freeholder, and the occupiers who have a 999 year lease. If this does not happen spontaneously as intermediate leaseholders decide that their interest does not warrant the trouble, it may be advisable to introduce a form of regulation that parallels the Leasehold Enfranchisement Acts.

Practicalities of valuation

Land value maps

Tony Vickers (2007:65) describes the way in which Lucas County Ohio has made publicly available an online map (Assessors Real Estate Information System, AREIS), showing up to date property valuation. This has improved the functioning of the property market, reduced the gap between the initial asking price for properties and the ultimate sale price; and has enabled people to report errors.

The New Land Market requires a database, linked to maps, that shows at least the current stewardship fees and Depreciated Replacement Cost for each site.

The meaning of these values for undeveloped sites are relatively easy to interpret, and the reasons for any differences in stewardship fees should be readily understandable in terms of acreage, location, socio-economic environment, planning permission, drainage, soil quality and so on.

The values of developed sites are, however, more difficult to interpret than in an ownership economy. A site may have very different stewardship fees from its apparently similar neighbour if one of them is encumbered with a restrictive covenant, different planning restrictions or a building that is either obsolescent or over-specified.

In a stewardship economy the maps will be scrutinised even more closely than similar maps in ownership economies as they document a liability to pay what will ultimately be 100 per cent of the market rent of each site. It will be important to make them freely available, and for the Land Stewardship Trust to engage in dialogue about the valuations.

The main source of disagreement with valuations in the New Land Market is likely to be about the Depreciated Replacement Cost of buildings and other improvements as there is no market mechanism to directly determine this value and it both determines the sale price of the owner's interest and influences the stewardship fees that a subsequent purchaser will be willing to bid.

There may be an appeal against the replacement cost, the depreciation factor or both. Appeals against the depreciation factor will be much rarer if a standardised rate of depreciation is used, as the only issue will be whether the building has been adequately maintained. Appeals against the replacement cost will require an independent valuer to assess this. These appeals will be rarer if there are very clear guidelines for the basis of calculating the Depreciated Replacement Cost.

Disputes over the market rent of land, whether this is unimproved land or land on which the Depreciated Replacement Cost of improvements has been agreed, are likely to be rare. The land values will be available on a publicly accessible geographic information system and will be directly determined every time a property is transferred on the open market. If is any disagreement about revaluation of the market rent of land between transfers, it can be challenged by offering the land on the market with the incumbent owner bidding what they think it is really worth.

Multiple interests

The valuation of a property in which there are multiple interests is based on the principle that the market rent of the whole property is made up of the sum of the market rents of each of its parts, with no consideration being given to marriage value.

These interests may be multiple owners, for example a block of flats. Here the Depreciated Replacement Cost of each flat is assessed, and flats are bought and sold independently in the new land market. For each flat stewardship fees are established in this transaction, or by comparison with similar transactions, and the market rent of the whole property is the sum of the market rents of all the flats.

The multiple interests may include some combination of leaseholds for each of which there is a market. Just as for the situation of multiple owners all the interests are identified, valued independently and added together.

Summary: This chapter has considered how, in a stewardship economy that makes use of the New Land Market, a steward who is taking over a property agrees to pay the Depreciated Replacement Cost of the improvements to the outgoing steward, and in addition makes the highest bid for the annual stewardship fees for the property. The key is to depreciate the building appropriately. If a building is depreciated too little, the building may become too valuable to demolish and the stewardship fees are too low. If it is depreciated too much then both construction and maintenance are discouraged.

An annual rate of depreciation of 2 per cent would reduce the real Depreciated Replacement Cost to half (in real terms) after about 35 years. If the inflation rate for replacement costs was 3 per cent then the nominal value of the improvements would increase by 1 per cent per year, or 40 per cent over 35 years, which could be politically acceptable.

The depreciation rate should be agreed at the design stage of a new building, taking into account quality of construction and anticipated running costs. Special arrangements for depreciation need to be made for historic and other unusual buildings, agricultural improvements, trees and other special cases.

The Depreciated Replacement Cost should follow the standard trajectory of depreciation until depreciation reaches 50 per cent, with no further depreciation until the building is judged not to be worth preserving. Any building that was poorly maintained would be depreciated further at the discretion of the valuer.

.

Chapter 8   Auction methods

The aims of an auction are to allocate an asset and to establish a price. This chapter discusses briefly the form of the auction that might be used in a stewardship economy.

Theory

All standard forms of auctions (including ascending, descending, first-price sealed bid, second-price sealed bids and 'all-pay') yield the same expected revenue, providing that certain conditions are met. These conditions may include risk-aversion, independence when bidding, equality of information, sufficiently large numbers of bidders and lack of collusion. This is known as the Revenue Equivalence Theorem (Paul Klemperer 2004:17).

Practice

The conditions of real auctions do not meet all the assumptions of the Revenue Equivalence Theorem. There have been many examples of auction fiascos including those for European 3G spectrum, TV franchises, electricity and company ownership (Paul Klemperer 2004:103), and these happen particularly when the number of bidders is relatively small. Paul Klemperer points out that each situation is different and there is no 'one size fits all' auction design (Paul Klemperer 2004:119). The most important factors in practical auction design are those encountered by any competition policy or anti-trust policy – how to prevent behaviour that deters entry, that is collusive or predatory. He shows that ascending auctions are vulnerable to collusion and may deter entry, and advocates greater use of a final 'sealed bid' stage at the end of an ascending auction – the 'Anglo-Dutch' auction.

Lessons from the 3G spectrum auctions

Current technology assumes that spectrum is a scarce resource. As devices incorporate more computer power and are able to distinguish between signals, it may be possible to manage at least some of the radio spectrum as 'open spectrum' where many operators can use the same spectrum. This would reduce the value of property rights to spectrum.

The spectrum auctions that took place in the UK in 2000 are described in detail by their chief auction theorist (Paul Klemperer 2004) and summarised in Stewardship Economy: private property without private ownership (Julian Pratt 2011: 21). Many other governments gifted spectrum to their national providers, thereby providing them with a subsidy. This may have given these providers an advantage in takeover battles in the international consolidation of the telecoms industry – or alternatively it may have made them less efficient as they have not been subjected to international competition.

A more significant criticism is that in retrospect the licences seemed overpriced. The telecoms companies, at the height of the dotcom boom, seriously overestimated short-term demand for 3G services. They found in retrospect that they had paid too much for the licences, their stock prices fell, and they had to reduce their levels of investment.

An important concern about the auction was whether paying fees for the licence would lead to higher charges for customers. The Radiocommunications Agency, the body responsible for conducting the auctions, argued that this would not happen – that bids are determined by the companies' expected levels of profits, and so by their business plans and the call charges they anticipate levying, not the other way around.

As the principal auction theorist advising the UK government on its 3G auction, Paul Klemperer (2004:209) argues that the phone companies lowered their expectations about market growth after the date of the auctions as a result of a change in the economic climate. The bids were made by the phone operators which, as entrepreneurs, make a wide range of business decisions and can be expected to know their own business better than any regulator.

Some features of the auctions did however exacerbate the overbidding. The 3G spectrum was auctioned in isolation at a time when the 2G spectrum was reaching capacity, so existing operators had no choice but to bid. The impact would have been less marked if there had been greater flexibility over the way that the whole spectrum is used or if the licences had been tradable, allowing the successful bidders to resell unwanted licences.

The ideal duration of the lease for spectrum is uncertain, and context-specific. It is clear that telecoms operators need a long timescale if they are to invest in making the best use of the spectrum. And the regulators would not want the hassle of frequent auctions. On the other hand, if the payments could have been determined at annual auctions and if, as in this case, the market rent subsequently fell, it would have been possible for the operator to bid lower annual payments in later years – provided that their investment in the network (their improvement) was protected if they were displaced at a later auction.

As the lessons from the spectrum auctions are applied to land it should be remembered that there are likely to be many bidders for most sites, and so the auctions are less likely to be problematic than the spectrum auctions. However, it will be important to give careful consideration to the choice of auction method to be used.

Online auctions

The internet auction site eBay has greatly increased the numbers of people engaging in auctions, and their familiarity with bidding behaviours. It uses a form of ascending price auction but with a fixed end time. This leads many bidders to make a bid in the last few seconds in what is effectively a final 'sealed bid' stage. For the purposes of this book, we could imagine property sales taking place using an online auction method of this sort.

Bidders in such an auction would need to go through a pre-qualification stage at which they pledge to pay, on successful completion of the auction, not just the amount bid as an annual stewardship fees but an immediate cash payment equal to the improvement value. It might be appropriate to require a deposit towards this, refundable if the bid is not successful.

Chapter 9   Where there are no land titles

This chapter describes the practical steps that could be taken to establish the market rent of land where there are no existing titles or claims to land and no existing market that determines rents. It describes a thought experiment which is introduced here before tackling the challenge of setting stewardship fees during transition from an established ownership economy (Chapter 10). A realistic proposal for transition in the UK is described elsewhere (Chapter 14).

There may be a few situations where stewardship could be, or could have been, introduced in more or less this way. In Eastern Europe in the early 1990s most land was owned by the state and and in order to return it to private tenure, there was an attempt to identify the families from whom it had been expropriated and to give it back to them. There would have been the opportunity here to introduce something like a Stewardship Economy and everyone would have benefited. Similar opportunities may present themselves in the future – for example in Cuba or Zimbabwe (Chapter 13). And if there was a desire to allocate property rights on the Moon this would be a good way to go about it.

This chapter describes one particular proposal – it could be modified in numerous ways within the spirit of stewardship.

Of the early advocates of raising taxes on the market rent of land, both Thomas Spence (1776) and Henry George (1879) advocated the immediate introduction of a tax of 100%. This would result in owners of land losing, overnight, the market value of their land. If there were no recognised land titles in existence, however, there might be no objection to such a transition. The necessary practical steps would be to set up a Land Stewardship Trust with a database of land holdings, estimate the Depreciated Replacement Cost of improvements on each site, establish a New

Land Market which determines both the new proprietor of any land that is transferred and its market rent, and sets up a mechanism for revaluaing land at least annually.

Land Stewardship Trust

A Land Stewardship Trust is created at national level to be responsible for the assessment and collection of stewardship fees. There is a political decision to be made as to whether this Trust is a government agency, a Commons Trust or put out to tender (in which case it may be a not-for profit corporation, a private corporation or take other organisational form such as a Blockchain).

Local outposts of the Land Stewardship Trust are established.

Database of land holdings

Each of the local outposts acquires information about all the sites (parcels of land) within its jurisdiction, building on information held by the existing owners and the national Land Registry.

It establishes a database linked to a map to form a Geographic Information System and an entry is made, for each interest in each site (both freehold and leasehold), that records the:

- unique (site) reference number
- location, boundaries and dimension of the site
- Registered Steward
- nature and duration of all interests (freehold, leasehold, mortgage)
- Depreciated Replacement Cost of improvements
- Registered Improvement Value of improvements
- Registered Disimprovement Value
- Registered stewardship fees
- current use
- any planning restrictions or permissions
- restrictive covenants and easements
- list of agreed comparables
- details of previous market transactions (improvement value, stewardship fees and date).

The maps and whole database are made freely available to any interested person or organisation.

Valuation

Each steward estimates the replacement cost of improvements such as buildings on the site and the depreciation factor, and from these calculates the Depreciated Replacement Cost. This is entered in the database, and the Registered Improvement Value set equal to it. The Land Stewardship Trust's quantity surveyor then verifies the valuation and adjusts it if necessary.

Stewardship fees

Once the Registered Improvement Value has been established as the agreed value of the steward's property, the steward becomes the registered steward of the land.

As a temporary measure the stewardship fees are set to zero and remain at zero until either the property is transferred on the open market or until the first annual revaluation takes place. Both of these events establish the stewardship fees to be paid.

New Land Market

Transfers

Secure tenure. A registered steward retains secure tenure provided they continue to pay their stewardship fees.

Bequests. The Land stewardship Trust simply alters the name of the Registered Steward in the database.

Open market sales. The Land Stewardship Trust inspects the property and makes any necessary change to the Registered Improvement Value, based on a rate of depreciation that is either standardised or individually assessed. It publicises the availability of the site and, after an interval of say 3 months, conducts an auction. Entry to the auction requires the winner to commit to paying the Registered Improvement Value to the outgoing steward. Bids are taken for the stewardship fees that the new steward will pay, and the highest bidder becomes the new steward of the site (and owner of the improvements).

Private transfers and gifts. If a steward wants to transfer a property to a particular person, without putting it on the open market, the two parties can agree any payment they like. The Land Stewardship Trust alters the name of the Registered Steward in the register without making any change to the Registered Improvement Value or the stewardship fees.

If many properties change hands in this way, reducing the number of open market sales for the Land Stewardship Trust to use as comparables, it might be necessary to withdraw this option. In this case the property would be auctioned in the usual way and the seller would be free to give the proceeds of the sale to the person in question.

If there are no bids at auction, the Land Stewardship Trust has the duty to find a steward to take responsibility for the land.

If it judges that the improvements have been correctly valued, the lack of bids means that no one thinks that the land can be used profitably. This could happen for a wide range of sorts of property – mountain, wilderness, a marginal farm particularly if it faces obligations to maintain biodiversity and landscape, property with a listed building that is very costly to keep up, a site with onerous planning restrictions or a burden of pollution and contamination. In this situation the Land Stewardship Trust could ask the planning body whether it judges it to be in the public interest to provide a subsidy to maintain and improve the property.

If a subsidy is provided, it would retain the original Registered Improvement Value and re-auction the property, indicating its willingness to take negative bids for Stewardship Support Fees (subsidies).

If the planning body does not consider it to be in the public interest to provide a subsidy, or there were still no (negative) bids, the improvements are overvalued (the estimated Depreciated Replacement Cost is higher than warranted). In this case the Land Stewardship Trust sets the stewardship fees at zero. It auctions the improvements to the highest bidder (up to the amount of the existing Registered Improvement Value). This sale value becomes the new Registered Improvement Value.

If the Registered Improvement Value is zero, the Land Stewardship Trust invites negative bids, Stewardship Support Fees, for the land (i.e.they offer to provide a subsidy to the steward who takes responsibility for the site). This ensures that all land has a steward.

Abandonment. If a registered steward wishes to abandon a site they inform the Land Stewardship Trust, which sets the Registered Improvement Value to zero and auctions the site.

Costs of the Land Stewardship Trust. The Land Stewardship Trust makes no charge to either buyer or seller. Its costs are paid from the total stewardship stewardship that it collects, before these are either remitted to government or distributed as a Universal Income. The sum is made public.

Annual revaluations

If a stewardship economy is to respond appropriately to changes in the economic climate, the valuations must be kept up to date, at least annually. It must be able to revalue all sites by comparison with comparables that have been recently exposed to the market, and there must be enough of these comparables.

On each anniversary of the date on which the stewardship was registered, the stewardship fee for each site is compared with recent market transactions of its comparables and its stewardship fees adjusted accordingly. The Land Stewardship Trust uses its Geographic Information System to make comparisons between sites.

- The Depreciated Replacement Cost is first increased by an index of building costs.

- If a landowner has improved the site in the last year they may register an increased replacement cost, and the Land Stewardship Trust needs to have a means of verifying this valuation.

- The Depreciated Replacement Cost is then calculated using an up-to-date depreciation factor for the building.

- Any site that may be subject to any form of damage, for example heavy metal pollution, is inspected periodically to assess the extent of any damage (disimprovement). The cost of the damage becomes the Registered Disimprovement Value. The steward can either clean the site up and apply for a new inspection or pay the Registered Disimprovement Value to the Land Stewardship Trust. Any steward who subsequently removes the disimprovement recoups the Registered Disimprovement Value.

The Land Stewardship Trust identifies comparables for each site. Ideally, a sufficient number of these comparables would be nominated in advance, and with the agreement of the steward, so that several comparables are exposed to the market each year. If, in any particular year, not enough comparables have been exposed then additional comparables need to be identified retrospectively.

The stewardship fees for each site are updated by comparing the site with comparables that have changed hands on the open market during the previous year. Initially this is by direct comparison. Once a site has itself been exposed to a market transaction, subsequent updates are by proportional comparison – the proportionate change in the value of the comparable is applied to the market rent of the index site at the time of its most recent exposure to the market.

There must be a mechanism for penalties to be applied to stewards who do not pay the stewardship fees. In the short run some flexibility could be introduced by allowing stewards to accumulate a debt, on which interest would be charged, up to a maximum of the unmortgaged part of the Registered Improvement Value. The debt would be repaid when the site next changed hands.

Beyond this the right to retain the stewardship of a property must be conditional on paying the stewardship fees. A stewardship economy requires a legal and police system capable of evicting non-payers of stewardship fees, auctioning the property and recovering unpaid fees.

Appeal by market mechanisms

If a steward feels they are paying higher stewardship fees than are warranted by current economic conditions they can appeal by asking the Land Stewardship Trust to put their property on the market and establish the stewardship fees directly at auction, at which they can bid what they think it is worth.

This chapter has outlined the essential steps a Land Stewardship Trust would need to take to make assessments of stewardship fees and handle property transactions. This approach could be applied during transition from an ownership economy in which there are no recognised prior claims to ownership of land. Transition from an established ownership economy builds on this approach and is described elsewhere (Chapter 10).

Part IV Environment

In ownership economies most environmental controls take the form of regulatory standards but increasing use has been made of the price mechanism and property rights, particularly tradable permits.

Quotas and permits have been introduced in ways that may be ineffective, inefficient and unfair:

- Ineffective – although a cap has been placed on environmental damage this has often allowed too much pollution or extraction

- Inefficient – when quotas and permits are not tradable there is no mechanism to ensure that damage reduction is carried out by whoever can do so at lowest cost

- Unfair – quotas and permits have generally been gifted to whoever is currently damaging the environment ('grandfathering').

A stewardship economy also makes extensive use of the price mechanism ; the general principles are discussed elsewhere. The environment is held in Trust by Environment Stewardship Trusts, one for each aspect of the environment. These Trusts may regulate the use of the environment but rely mainly on the price mechanism and property rights to do so.

Part IV takes one example of how to manage the environment and contrasts the flaws of the European Emissions Trading Scheme with the approach taken in a stewardship economy. Here auctioning permits would be both efficient and fair, although the political challenge of setting an effective cap on emissions would be just as great as in an ownership economy.

Chapter 10   Tradable permits

One of our major challenges is how to avoid climate change by managing greenhouse gas emissions.

In an ownership economy environmental resources may be managed as private property, common property or collective property. Each of these forms of property rights would be found in a stewardship economy, but the nature of these rights is radically different. Allocating environmental resources to private individuals and corporations has in ownership economies allowed these private owners to capture the resource rent provided by these resources.

In a stewardship economy the environment, like the land, is the common property of humankind. It may be leased to individuals and corporations, but resource rents are collected for the common good. This may be achieved by environmental taxation, but the auction of tradable permits is a better option. It seems that all a regulator has to do is to decide the acceptable rate of emissions within its jurisdiction, issue the appropriate number of permits each year and ensures that they are surrendered when carbon is emitted. But the devil is in the detail. This chapter takes the example of the way in which carbon permits have been handled in the European Union Emissions Trading Scheme (EUETS) and contrasts this with the way they should be handled in a stewardship economy.

The European emissions trading scheme

The Kyoto Protocol (1997) led the European Union to set up the European Union Emissions Trading Scheme (EU ETS) in 2005, the first and largest multilateral action taken to reduce greenhouse emissions and the largest carbon market. The essential elements of this cap and trade scheme are:

- The scheme is designed to cover the 11,500 major industrial users of energy – the electricity generation stations and major users of fossil fuels that account for 16 billion tonnes per year of CO2 (45 per cent of Europe's output).

- The regulator sets an annual cap for permitted carbon emissions and issues permits equivalent to 45 per cent of this cap, with the rest emitted by minor emitters and individuals. Each permit allow the emission of 1 tonne of CO2 or equivalent greenhouse gas.

- These permits are allocated amongst the energy users – in the early years as a gift but with an increasing proportion allocated by auction.

- The energy users have to surrender a permit for each tonne of CO2 they emit. They can sell any permits that they do not need or save them for the future. If they emit more than their allocation of permits they must buy them in the market.

Design choices

The designers of the EU ETS faced a number of choices in designing this system, including:

- The number of permits to allocate each year (the size of the cap).

- Where in the economy to apply the requirement for permits.

- How to allocate the permits amongst the energy users.

- How the EU ETS should interact with low-consumption countries that are not part of the scheme.

- How to gain political acceptance.

- How the scheme should develop over the years to reduce the cap and extend to include a greater proportion of greenhouse emissions.

Number of permits to issue each year

It is not self-evident how much greenhouse gas we should emit this year, next year, and on into the future. There are three rather different approaches to thinking about this:

Science

A direct way to use scientific understanding, derived from observation and computer modelling, would be to make a judgment about the maximum acceptable level of climate change and to take whatever steps are needed to reduce the levels of greenhouse gas emissions so that there is a good chance that this is achieved.

George Monbiot (2006:15) advocated a target maximum temperature rise of 2°C above pre-industrial levels on the grounds that this is the point at which significant impacts are expected to occur and also the point at which critical positive feedback loops may come into play. This is the level that was accepted at the Paris agreement (2016).

Greenhouse gas emissions are measured in ppm CO2e (the concentration of greenhouse gases equivalent to the number of parts per million of carbon dioxide). Total greenhouse gas levels have risen from 280 ppm CO2e before the industrial revolution to 430 ppm CO2e in 2007 (Nicholas Stern 2007:193) and are currently rising at 2.5 ppm CO2e per year. Nicholas Stern (2007:220) reviewed a range of models and suggested that stabilising greenhouse gases at 550ppm CO2e would provide a worse than 1 in 4 chance of stabilising the global temperature rise at under 2°C.

Stabilising at 450 ppm CO2e would give a roughly 50:50 chance of staying below a 2°C rise (above pre-industrial levels). To stabilise at this level, global net emissions would have to have stopped rising by 2017 and then would have to fall from this peak by at least 5 per cent per year, reaching 30 per cent of 2007 emission rates by 2050 (Nicholas Stern 2007:218).

The advantage of an approach based purely on science is that the logic is clear and transparent, which is important if people are to be asked to make short-term sacrifices.

Economics

An economic approach builds on the scientific one. Rather than simply making a judgment about the tolerable level of climate change, it weighs up the benefits and costs of different alternatives. Stabilising at 450 ppm CO2e would probably cost about three times more than stabilising at 550 ppm CO2e, for example, as it involves replacing industrial plant immediately rather than waiting till it reaches the end of its useful life (Nicholas Stern 2007:276). So which course of action should we choose?

The Stern review weighs the costs and the benefits of reducing (abating) greenhouse gas emissions to arrive at its recommendations for how much greenhouse gas we should emit. This approach requires both technical climate models and economic models of the costs of abatement and the costs of possible future climates, appropriately weighted by their probabilities. It has the problem of all cost-benefit studies that it can be very difficult to put a price on many benefits and costs. There are also major uncertainties about the probabilities that should be attached to unlikely but catastrophic futures. There is a challenge about how much value should be placed on a human life (the 'value of a statistical life'); this should surely be equal for all humans in the context of a global problem, even though orthodox economics assigns people a lower value if they live in a low-consumption economy as they are less productive. And above all these calculations are highly dependent on how important the future is deemed to be compared with the present, the discount rate .

This economic approach led Nicholas Stern to recommend that we aim to stabilise at 500 - 550ppm CO2e (Nicholas Stern 2007:652). He suggested that this would incur an immediate cost of 1 per cent of global GDP ($600bn) and prevent a 5 per cent loss in global GDP that would result from climate change.

George Monbiot (2006:49) rejected the proposition that the costs and benefits of reducing CO2 emissions can be considered to be commensurable and argues that the case for action rests on the moral assertion that people and places have intrinsic value that cannot be weighed against the costs of action.

Politics

In spite of these forays into rationality and ethics, a survey of climate change by the Economist (2006:17) concluded that the economics are so uncertain that politicians will have to decide. If they use a 'cap and trade' system this means that they have to decide the number of permits to auction each year. This locates the decision in the 'art of the possible', a position reflected in the Paris agreement (2016) at which a welcome agreement was reached that we must keep temperature rises below 2°C and should aim for 1.5°C. The proposed mechanism, however, is to exhort individual states to try a bit harder.

Where to apply the requirement for permits

The requirement to buy and surrender permits may be imposed 'upstream', 'midstream' or 'downstream'.

Upstream

Here the firm that introduces fossil fuels into the economy, or other greenhouse gases into the atmosphere, is required to surrender permits equal to the amount of greenhouse gases that will ultimately be released. This includes:

- fossil fuel extraction (61 per cent of emissions)
- deforestation (18 per cent)
- agriculture (including methane) (14 per cent)
- cement and chemicals (3 per cent)

(if the agreement is not global) importing fossil fuels, and indeed any goods and services that have given rise to greenhouse gas emissions in their production.

The purpose of upstream permits is to set a True Cost Price that reflects the social and environmental damage that will be caused by climate change . As the cost of carbon is passed through the economy it will increase the cost of all goods and services that result in carbon emissions.

The advantage of upstream permits is that they are administratively relatively simple and unobtrusive as few firms have to purchase the permits, reducing regulatory costs. All other firms, and consumers, simply respond to price signals.

The disadvantage of an upstream approach is that the small numbers of buyers may behave in a collusive way so that auctions for permits do not realise their true market value and the cost of carbon emissions is underpriced. This is a challenge that is familiar from the spectrum auctions and highlights the importance of countering monopolistic behaviour by anti-trust legislation and thoughtful auction design. The problem might be reduced if environmental groups were also able to bid for these permits so that they could retire them in their effort to curb carbon emissions faster than the regulator considers necessary. But if a cartel did develop and proved difficult to disrupt. it would be necessary to move permits further downstream so that firms, or even individuals, have the responsibility to buy and surrender permits.

Mid-stream

The requirement for permits may be applied 'mid-stream', the approach taken by the European Union Emissions Trading Scheme (EUETS). This imposes the duty to buy and surrender emissions permits on major industrial users of energy. This has the advantage that there are enough companies to establish a market free from collusive behaviour when permits are auctioned. One of its disadvantages is the cost to government, firms and ultimately taxpayers and consumers of administering the scheme and ensuring compliance by all the firms involved. Another is that this mid-stream approach applies to less than half the CO_2 emitted in Europe.

Downstream

Alternatively, the requirement to surrender permits might be applied 'downstream', to all those organisations and households that use energy derived from burning fossil fuels or release greenhouse gases directly.

How to allocate the permits

Auction

The designers of the EU ETS recognised that in an ideal world all emissions permits would be auctioned. This approach provides the best opportunity for a True Cost Price to be established for greenhouse gas emissions. This price is passed on to the whole economy, leading to changes in the behaviour of both producers and consumers.

However, if permits had been auctioned from the outset this would have instantly transferred the whole burden of paying for pollution to the polluters, confiscating the free use of the environment upon which their businesses has been based. In deregulated markets there is nothing to stop firms from passing the costs on to their customers – indeed it is the purpose of permits to put a True Cost Price on carbon. But there are at least two major problems with this approach. One is that European producers are competing in a global market, where their higher prices would make them less competitive. The other is that in a regulated market, such as the one for electricity, the regulatory body might not allow prices to rise, in which case the firms would have become less profitable. Industry lobbyists argued successfully that auctioning permits would cause firms to go out of business.

Gifting to existing polluters

So, in the EU ETS, permits were not auctioned but given to existing polluters – an approach known as 'grandfathering'. Member states were permitted to auction 5 per cent of permits in Phase I (2005-2007), increasing in later phases, but almost all started by gifting them.

It might be expected that if a company is able to meet the abatement (reduction) target, equal to the number of permits that it has been given, it would have no additional costs to pass on to consumers. But it has not worked out like that. Regulators set energy prices in a way that is complex but includes an element that ensures a 'fair return on capital'. Energy companies have been gifted valuable property rights which form part of their capital, and they require extra income to offset the opportunity cost of holding them (the income they could obtain by investing their value in some other way). Electricity companies increased their prices to make their customers pay the value of the permits – in spite of the fact that they themselves did not have to pay anything but received them as a gift (Jos Sijm 2005:88). In addition, the over-allocation of permits means that many companies made a profit from selling un-needed permits.

The consultancy CE Delft have calculated that windfall profits from the EU ETS from 2008 to 2014 amounted to a total of € 8 billion from over-allocation and € 15 billion from pass-through to customers (€ 2 billion in the UK). The new allocation mechanism from 2013 was thought unlikely to result in any loss of subsidy (Sander de Bruyn et al 2016).

Low-Consumption Economies and emissions offsetting

Clean Development Mechanism

Cap and trade can be a very efficient way of reducing greenhouse gas emissions because energy users who can easily reduce their energy use will do so and sell their surplus permits to users who would find it more expensive to reduce their use. Across the economy, it ensures that emissions reductions occur where they can be most easily and cheaply achieved.

This only works within the states participating in an emissions trading scheme. There are many examples where emissions reduction in low-consumption economies can be achieved at much lower levels of investment than within the European Union. In order to draw low-consumption economies into the international challenge of emissions reduction, the designers of the EU ETS included a carbon offsetting scheme called the Clean Development Mechanism.

Firms in Europe that want to emit greenhouse gases in greater quantities than the emissions permits they hold have the option to 'offset' these emissions by buying credits from low-consumption economies. These credits fund reductions in net CO_2 emissions by 'Clean Development Mechanism' projects in these counties, which are thereby drawn into the Kyoto protocol as beneficiaries. In the first year, European countries paid producers in low-consumption economies \$2.7 billion to reduce their emissions by about 374 million tons of CO_2 equivalent – about 5 per cent of total emissions.

This approach is notoriously open to malpractice and fraud, particularly by paying firms for changes that they would have made anyway. The beneficiaries are firms in low-consumption economies and the firms based in high-consumption economies that inspect and verify offsetting – not the ordinary people in low-consumption economies. But even if it has done no more than highlight the need for transfers from high-consumption to low-consumption economies, which is necessary in any fair future, it will have served a useful purpose.

Voluntary offsetting

One interesting development, which suggests that there is some public support for a bolder approach to greenhouse emissions, is the growth in voluntary offsetting. Some people have chosen to offset at least some of their emissions – for example their air travel and/or car travel. Some companies have chosen to become 'carbon neutral' in their business, or at least in some aspect of their business, by buying carbon credits to offset their emissions.

Gaining political acceptance

Grandfathering the permits was a key factor in the complex task of gaining political acceptance across the member states. It bought the support of the existing polluting firms. And if permits had been auctioned this would have been deemed to be a revenue-raising measure and would have failed to gain the unanimous approval by EU member states this requires.

It is not hard to understand why governments have felt that the only way they can get acceptance for a system of carbon emission permits is to give them away to powerful business interests. But there are no shortages of proposals for how they could be issued in a more equitable way.

At an international level the Global Commons Institute has long advocated sharing out the permits to governments in proportion to their population size.

The Foundation for the Economics of Sustainability advocates what it calls 'cap and share' (FEASTA 2008:3). In this variant of 'cap and trade' each national climate protection trust distributes an equal number of pollution authorisation permits to each adult resident, who can then either destroy them or sell them through post offices and banks.

This proposal would provide everyone with an income that is clearly derived from the 'global commons' and which does not pass through the hands of the government. It could turn the resistance to environmental charges that comes from their impact on the cost of living, particularly for the very poorest, into popular support. It would also remove the subsidy the energy companies enjoy as first occupiers of the resource – with the wealth inequalities and potential for conflict that this causes.

Extending the scope of the ETS

The designers of the EU ETS were well aware of its limitations, particularly the problem that many sources of greenhouse gas emissions were outside its scope and were keen to extend its scope.

Short-lived climate pollutants including methane, hydrofluorocarbons (HFCs), black carbon and tropospheric ozone are managed through regulation outside the EU Emissions Trading System. The most important areas that have needed extension of the EU ETS are emissions caused by aviation and shipping.

Aviation

Air travel has always been provided with a generous government subsidy compared with other forms of transport because the countries that set up the International Civil Aviation Organisation agreed in 1944 that no tax would be levied on aviation fuel for international flights. And air travel was excluded from the Kyoto protocol, a disaster for the environment as one person flying from London to New York and back causes about the same amount of CO2 emissions as the average person in the EU does in heating their home for a year.

Aviation contributes 2 per cent of global CO2 emissions, but simply accounting for the number of tonnes of CO2 released is insufficient. The impact of aviation on climate change, its radiative forcing due to other pollutants, is 2 to 4 times greater than would be predicted simply from the amount of CO2 released, not including its additional impact on the formation of cirrus clouds (IPCC 1999:9), though this effect is more localised and of shorter duration than the CO2. The price of aviation fuel needs to reflect its impact on the climate as the number of tonnes of carbon dioxide equivalent (CO2e) not simply of CO2.

The intention had always been to extend the EU ETS to commercial aviation, and this took place in January 2012 for flights within the EU.

The International Civil Aviation Organisation (ICAO) agreed in 2016 to adopt carbon offsetting to reduce international aviation emissions – the first agreement to reduce emissions in a global sector. Airlines will buy 'emission units' generated by projects that reduce CO2 emissions. This reflects an aspirational goal of achieving carbon neutral growth from 2020, and a commitment to using market mechanisms. All European states will participate, and this will be their contribution to reducing the impact that aviation has on climate change.

The success of this approach will depend on the price of the emission units, the Global Market-Based Measure (GMBM).

The UK government has supported the development of a well-designed international emissions trading scheme for aviation – but the European emissions trading scheme goes only a small way towards becoming a well-designed scheme. The support of the aviation industry has been bought by 'grandfathering' carbon permits to existing airlines, which it was anticipated to hand them new profits of around £1bn per year as they pass on the price of the permits to their customers (Dagmar Nelissen & Jasper Faber 2012:5). The rhetoric of limiting greenhouse gas emissions from aviation is anyway barely credible in the light of plans to increase airport capacity to allow the number of airline passengers passing through the UK to more than double by 2030.

Shipping

Carbon Dioxide from shipping contributes 2.6% to global CO_2 emissions, and black carbon is also important. If shipping were a country it would be the sixth largest emitter, more than Germany. And emissions are still rising in spite of energy efficiency gains due to increased traffic and speed (Naya Olmer et al 2017). Shipping emissions were not included in the Paris agreement and, like aviation, are challenging to control because they are beyond the ability of a single country, or even the European Union, to tackle alone.

The International Maritime Organisation (IMO) has expressed the ambition to reduce greenhouse gas emissions by 50 per cent from 2008 to 2050 but they appear to be relying mainly on innovation in fuel and propulsion. Meanwhile they have required large (but not other) ships to monitor and report their annual CO_2 emissions from 2018.

Forests

The role of forests in carbon sequestration is not simple. A mature natural forest, in which new growth is balanced by decay, is broadly carbon neutral. Deforestation releases CO_2 into the atmosphere, while new forests sequester it while they are growing. Sequestration can be very long term if timber is extracted and used for construction and manufacture of items that are long-lived.

It is understandable, therefore, that the global community wants to limit deforestation, which may account for 10 – 20 per cent of the carbon emitted during the 1990s (Economist 2004:11). But it is also unreasonable for high-consumption economies to deny to low-consumption economies in the tropics the immediate financial benefits of logging and agriculture.

Several forest nations have taken major steps to protect their forests. For example, 44 per cent of the Amazon region of Brazil is protected as park or reserve, enforced using satellite imagery

(Economist 2014: 55). Mexico has provided income support for forest organisations. Democratic opposition to deforestation, and the defence of the rights of indigenous people, has had a positive impact.

Forest nations that act in the interests of the global community need some form of international subsidy. Peru approaches this by selling 'conservation concessions' to groups committed to managing the forest sustainably. This ensures that its economy benefits financially when deforestation is avoided.

The Clean Development Mechanism includes the planting of new forest. It may be expedient to extend this to include projects that prevent deforestation.

Carbon capture and storage

There is interest from the private sector, as well as government, in an approach that is complementary to emission abatement – the sequestration of greenhouse gases such as methane and CO_2. It is possible to capture CO_2 from, for example, power stations and store it indefinitely beneath the ground or the sea bed. If this proves to be feasible on a commercial scale this is one of a range of innovative businesses that will have been called into existence by the true cost pricing of carbon. At present this technology probably needs a development subsidy as it is languishing due to the absurdly low price of carbon.

Lessons from the EU emissions trading scheme

The EU emissions trading scheme has many undesirable consequences (FEASTA (2006:1):

Number of permits issued each year

The scheme has set an unrealistically low price for carbon emissions because lobbying by governments ensured that the total European 'cap' was set well above current emissions. The original intention was to cap emissions at the then current levels by issuing the appropriate number of permits. But national governments lobbied on behalf of their national CO_2 producers, and the European Union responded by issuing more permits.

Permits to emit a tonne of CO2 traded at €34 at their peak in 2006, a level that should be high enough to begin to change the behaviour of people and firms even though it is lower than it needs to be to halt climate change. Once the overallocation was recognised, however, the price of carbon on the EU ETS collapsed to around €1 per tonne in 2007 (Economist 2007 (b)).

The allocation for 2008-12 was reduced and carbon price futures rose but during the Great Recession that followed the financial crash of 2008 demand for energy fell, and in 2011 carbon prices were still too low to stimulate the necessary behaviour change.

In 2014 the European Union decided to reduce the number of permits in circulation, and so drive up their price, by introducing delays in the auctioning of new permits, placing them in the Market Stability Reserve (MSR) – a mountain of permits. Carbon prices rose to about €7 per tonne in 2017.

The intention had always been to reduce the cap on carbon emissions (the total number of permits) each year. This has not been enough to mop up the surplus of permits, let alone raise the price of carbon to change behaviour. The annual rate of reduction will be increased from 1.7% to 2.4% from 2021.

Limited requirement for permits

Requirement for permits is incomplete – it covers less than half the total emissions as it does not apply to the home, road transport or smaller energy users. There are many greenhouse gases that it does not cover.

The scheme is more expensive to administer and police than upstream permits.

Unfair means of allocation

Customers pay while the major polluting firms profit. Property rights in the natural world are given to polluting firms, who take the profits and pass the costs of limiting climate change on to consumers.

The ultimate aim should be for all permits to be auctioned. Annual gifting of about €16 billion in permits will continue, though these will be re-focused on sectors that are most at risk of relocating outside the European Union.

There is a danger that these property rights may become entrenched, and the scheme fails to provide a fair basis for sharing emissions between European states. It has missed the opportunity to signal that the right way allocate emissions rights between states is on an equal per capita basis, even if this might take some time to achieve. Instead, the right to emit CO_2 in Europe may remain rooted in past patterns of pollution. Or it may move towards a needs-based approach. If that happens each country will argue that it needs more than its equal per capita share of the permits because it has a greater need for heating, or cooling, or water, or building or whatever.

It is open to corrupt behaviour by national governments, which are responsible for dividing their total allocation between their domestic producers and may do so in response to lobbying by industry. Governments may later fail to monitor the whole of a firm's emissions.

Adverse incentives

The scheme encourages producers to keep polluting plants open as a firm loses the permits it was allocated for a plant if this is closed.

It hinders the switch to renewable energy by subsiding new electricity generation plants to use fossil fuel through the gift of emissions permits to their operators.

It distorts markets by subsidising large energy users and penalising their smaller and greener competitors.

The future

In spite of all these problems the EU emissions trading scheme has taken a first step towards the introduction of private property rights to CO_2 emissions. Grandfathering is being phased out, and more that 50 per cent of permits are now allocated at auction. The scheme enables emissions to be reduced at the least cost. It has made a small difference through price increases and emissions offsetting. It has resulted in the development of markets for current and future permits and remains the European Union's main instrument for achieving its 2030 target.

In summary, lessons from the European Union Emissions Trading Scheme are:

- An effective scheme needs to include all greenhouse gas emissions, not just the CO2 emitted by major energy users.

- The cap has to be set independently from the influence of lobbying by the private sector.

- Even if there needs to be a transition period, any scheme needs to move as fast as possible to fully auctioned allocation.

- In the absence of a global emissions trading scheme, interaction with states outside the scheme needs to be carefully considered.

Stewardship economy and the environment

In a stewardship economy the underlying principles are that the natural world is held on behalf of humankind by Stewardship Trusts, which create private use-rights;   and that whoever has these rights compensates others by paying fees that are determined by market mechanisms.   This process allows the market to establish a True Cost Price for carbon – a price the reflects not just normal production costs but the cost its of environmental and social damage.

An Atmosphere Stewardship Trust (Sky Trust) would be responsible for the atmosphere as a sink for greenhouse gases and would exercise this responsibility by conducting annual auctions for emissions permits (Julian Pratt 2021: Chapter 7).

Alternative forms of tradable permits

The underlying principles of stewardship do not prescribe a particular form for a stewardship economy, but a range of possible economies.

One choice is the role of the state, and this choice would determine whether the Atmosphere Stewardship Trust was an agency of the state, a Commons Trust or a private sector franchise.

More important is the choice of the form that the permits take. The simplest approach would be to auction upstream permits each year and distribute the revenue as an Environmental Dividend. Other approaches that have been proposed and are compatible with stewardship are Cap and Share and Personal Carbon Allowances.

Number of permits to issue each year

Climate change is a global problem that requires global solutions. Ideally an international Sky Trust or its regulator would set an annual carbon budget – the total number of permits for greenhouse gas emissions for each year. It might auction permits directly; or allocate permits to each country in proportion to its population, with each country auctioning its own permits.

In a stewardship economy, a global regulatory body would ideally decide the annual 'carbon budget' – the number of permits for greenhouse gas emissions – using either scientific, economic or political logic. This cap needs to be achievable and believable. If a global body cannot command the necessary respect, national and international bodies need to assume their (per capita) share of the responsibility.

Where to apply the requirement for permits-
Upstream permits with Environmental Dividend

This approach requires firms who extract fossil fuels or otherwise introduce carbon into the economy to surrender permits that they have purchased, either at auction or in a secondary market. This increases the cost of fossil fuels, and this cost is passed on through the economy to consumers.

The Sky Trust distributes the revenue from these auctions (after it has deducted its own running costs) as an equal per capita Environmental Dividend to the whole population covered by the agreement. As a consequence, wealth is redistributed from individuals with a large carbon footprint to those with a small carbon footprint. In the UK, 20 per cent of people on low incomes have no car and 50 per cent don't fly.

Cap and Share

The New Economics Foundation in collaboration with FEASTA have proposed that upstream permits should be given to everyone on an equal per capita basis. They would then be free to sell them through any intermediaries they chose, which would establish a true cost price for carbon. In financial terms this has exactly the same effect as auctioning permits and distributing an Environmental Dividend. It is a more cumbersome process but the symbolism of giving everyone their share of the carbon budget to do what they like with (including destroying it) is a powerful act and fully compatible with stewardship.

Personal Carbon Allowances

The best-know form of Personal Carbon Allowance is the Tradable Energy Quota (TEQ) (David Fleming 2007). This is a downstream permit which people would have to surrender whenever they pay for fuel – petrol, diesel, natural gas, coal, electricity.

Forty per cent of the carbon budget would be distributed equally to all adults as TEQs (to reflect the current situation where 40 per cent of carbon is currently emitted as the result of the use of fuel by individuals and households). Households that use less than their quota could sell their excess permits to those that use more than their quota. Sixty per cent of the carbon budget is auctioned to firms that use energy, who pass on the cost of the permits on to their customers as higher prices.

Personal Carbon Allowances would have the same impact on the distribution of wealth as auctioning permits and distributing an Environmental Dividend, provided that the revenue from the auctions and payments for use of the other 60 per cent of the carbon budget was also distributed on an equal per capita basis.

TEQs have several advantages over upstream permits. Every household and every organisation (including small businesses, charities, government agencies) has to account for the greenhouse gas emissions caused by their direct energy consumption. Having a clear personal carbon quota would focus people's thinking and engage people directly with the struggle to cut greenhouse gas emissions. Many people would be likely to live within their quota as a matter of pride, not just as a response to a financial carrot and stick. And the allocation of the Tradable Energy Quotas would be transparent and demonstrably fair, whereas people might not trust the Sky Trust to distribute all its revenue as Environmental Dividend.

TEQs and other downstream approaches have the disadvantage that they would be expensive to administer – perhaps £1-2 billion a year (DEFRA 2008:5), although this has been challenged – and the possibilities for fraud and corruption would be significant.

Downstream permits may not be a good way to tackle multiple environmental issues at the same time. Even having to surrender separate permits for both energy and the water embedded in a product would be complicated, though digital wallets allow holders to spend multiple currencies simultaneously.

How to allocate permits

There are two possible mechanisms for allocating permits in a stewardship economy. One is to auction the permits and distribute the revenue as an Environmental Dividend. The other is to distribute the permits themselves on an equal per capita basis, enabling individuals to use or to sell them in the market.

Emissions offsetting

Protecting low-consumption economies

Bjørn Lomberg (2001:322) points out that those who will suffer most from climate change are the poorest people in low-consumption economies who are liable to flooding and extreme weather – but that these people are dying today because of a lack of income that could be provided by economic growth. He argues that money would be better spent on development programmes that have clear benefits now, rather than on climate change abatement with its possible future benefits.

These are not necessarily mutually exclusive objectives. In a stewardship economy where there are international agreements about environmental stewardship, the dilemma disappears. The global revenue from the sale of carbon permits would be distributed to countries in proportion to their population. This compensates people in low-consumption economies for the current imbalance in emissions, while still providing incentives for them to keep their emissions low. A country might use its revenue to provide an equal per capita Environmental Dividend, or it might use it for collective investment in development – in adapting to climate change, in agriculture or in the Millennium Development Goals. The more strenuously we tackle climate change, the higher the price of carbon permits and the more wealth we transfer to low-consumption economies.

Where Low-Consumption Economies act in the global interest they need to be compensated financially. Ecuador set up a legally binding Trust in 2010 to leave 1 billion barrels of oil in the ground in Yasun National Park and asked for donations from philanthropists and from other countries of $3.6 billion (John Vidal and Rory Carroll 2010).

There are special issues for Low-Consumption Economies in transition from an ownership economy. Under the Kyoto protocol, firms in low -consumption economies do not have to buy emissions permits but benefit from the funding of clean development mechanism projects by firms in high-consumption economies. During transition to stewardship, before low-consumption economies take on the same status as high-consumption economies in carbon trading, these transfers would need to continue and would be funded by the revenue that would otherwise be paid as the Environmental Dividend for that country.

Carbon capture

If an industry captures CO2 and sequesters it permanently, the Sky Trust rewards it by paying the current market value of the permits that would be required to emit that amount of CO2. This provides the carbon capture industry with an income stream, though the magnitude is unpredictable while market prices of carbon permits are volatile.

Preventing deforestation

In a similar way the Sky Trust could reward Forest Nations that do not destroy their forest, though the right level of reward is not so clear. The Sky Trust might estimate the burden of greenhouse gases that each country is capable of releasing by deforestation each year and agree to pay for that number of permits at market rates, on condition that the deforestation does not occur.

Gaining political acceptance

Supporters of environmental taxes and charges have generally advocated using them to replace harmful taxes, but the general population does not trust the state to do so. This has allowed their opponents to portray them as stealth taxes.

If the state can be sufficiently disciplined to use the whole of the revenue from environmental taxes and charges to pay an equal per capita Environmental Dividend, these could gain political acceptance. People using less than their fair (equal) share of the environment would gain, as their payments would be less than their Environmental Dividend. And even those using more than their fair share should be able to see the fairness of compensating the low users.

Who benefits?

Present or future generations?

In an established economy the revenue from the auction of permits (or the revenue from carbon taxes) should be used for the benefit of future generations, to mitigate or adapt to climate change. Stewardship Economy proposes, in the case of greenhouse gases and for tactical reasons, an indefinite transition to this arrangement during which the whole of the revenue from the auction of emissions permits is distributed to those now living on an equal basis as an Environmental Dividend.

Under this arrangement someone who uses exactly their fair share of fossil fuels finds that they are neither worse-off nor better-off than they would be if they were living in an ownership economy – their Environmental Dividend exactly balances the increase in costs. People who use more than their fair share of the carbon budget are worse off, as they pay out in higher prices more than they receive in Environmental Dividend. (This bears unfairly on tenants whose landlords have not insulated their properties effectively, which needs to be tackled by regulation or subsidies). People who use less than their fair share are better off, and this ensures that they have a reason to support the scheme out of self-interest. Everyone still has a financial incentive to reduce their own carbon consumption.

Polluters or people?

When permits are given ('grandfathered') to existing polluters this transfers wealth from the government and its people to polluters. On the other hand, when governments auction the permits (or give them to the people) we should all benefit. Ownership economies are quite capable of allocating time-limited property rights by auction – the spectrum auctions are an example. But they have only ever done so when this does not challenge an historical claim by powerful interests.

Emissions permits work by ensuring that the cost of climate change is reflected in the prices of products that have been responsible for greenhouse gas emissions. Firms have to be free to pass on the full costs of the permits all the way down the chain of production – this is not an accident but the mechanism by which true cost pricing works.

Political possibilities

Local initiatives

Some people have already changed their behaviours, either as consumers or as producers. Behaviour change is most likely to happen in community, and local attempts to make a transition to a low-carbon economy such as the Transition Town movement have provided a great deal of support (Rob Hopkins 2009:93-

103). These efforts will need to continue in a stewardship economy.

National governments

It seems that the best hope for combating climate change in the immediate future is at a national level. The difficulty is that any state that unilaterally imposes True Cost Pricing for carbon, or indeed regulatory controls on greenhouse gas emissions, risks making its businesses uncompetitive.

International agreementt

We really do need the ambitious goals of the Paris agreement to be translated into action, particularly on carbon pricing, that does not penalise the trading position of those who undertake it.

A stewardship economy would help

The use of upstream permits in a stewardship economy would ensure that 100 per cent of the carbon introduced into the economy is subject to emissions trading and is administratively simpler than the mid-stream permits of the European Union ETS.

Allocation by auction in a stewardship economy, with the revenue distributed as an Environmental Dividend, is fairer than the EU ETS as the costs fall ultimately on people who are responsible for more than their fair share of emissions rather than on all consumers.

Indeed, in a stewardship economy people who are responsible for less than their fair share of emissions receive a net income from the Environmental Dividend – and this includes people in low-consumption economies.

Part V   Transition to Stewardship

So far this book has described what a steady-state stewardship economy might be like and how it could be introduced where there are no recognised prior claims to ownership of the natural world. Part V discusses how existing ownership economies could make a transition to stewardship.

Where there is a political desire for land reform, transition to stewardship would provide a fair and affordable way to carry it out (Chapter 13).

Transition from an established ownership economy requires the collection of only the increase in market rent that occurs after the onset of transition (Chapter 11). Here there are political challenges, because millions of individuals own land and none of us would be keen to recognise any dilution of our ownership rights. But we might choose to embark on a gradual transition if the benefits outweigh the costs for most of us. This is difficult to imagine in times of rapidly rising house prices but is easier to consider when people are aware of the risks of falling house prices and negative equity. Gradual transition will be necessary: a rapid transition to a stewardship economy would amount to confiscation of the land value which would be unacceptable. Transition would probably be at least 50 per cent complete within 25 years of the start of transition (Chapter 11).

Transition to stewardship for the environment is potentially more straightforward than for land, as many rights to the environment are still held as collective property or as open access regimes (Chapter 13) and there would be less opposition from existing private owners.

This Part V also considers how best to use the revenue from stewardship fees during transition (Chapter 11) and the possible international consequences of unilateral transition to stewardship (Chapter 14).

Chapter 11 Introducing Stewardship Fees

There are many ways in which it would be possible to introduce stewardship fees into an established ownership economy. What is needed is an approach that sufficiently respects the property rights of existing landowners while moving steadily towards full implementation.

Most contemporary advocates of these ideas accept that the immediate introduction of stewardship fees (Chapter 8) would be too harsh and suggest a phased introduction over the course of ten years or so).

John Stuart Mill (1848 Book V Chapter 2 Section 5: 361-2) proposed respecting the right of existing owners to retain the value of their existing property rights by imposing a 100 per cent tax but limiting this to future increases in market rent. This is the approach taken in Stewardship economy: private property without private ownership.

This chapter begins by describing a broad approach to transition that builds on the situation where there are no pre-existing property rights (Chapter 8). The way this might play out in practice is set out for residential and non-residential land (Chapter 14) and for the environment (Chapter 13).

If we want to get to a stewardship economy we would not choose to start from an established ownership economy. How much easier it would have been if we had made this transition centuries, or even decades, ago. The greatest difficulties lie not with introducing stewardship but with rolling back the complexities of the current system of tax and benefits.

But we have no choice about where to start and indeed it is only very recently that it has become possible to maintain a register of up-to-date valuations and to put in place practical methods for the valuation of land when this is subject to stewardship fees that are 100 per cent of the market rent.

Principles for transition

Transition to stewardship from an ownership economy may take place in many ways. If stewardship is to be a practical radical proposal that would benefit us all, rather than a revolutionary aspiration that would almost certainly harm those who always suffer most from change, the poorest, there are some general principles to which transition should conform (Stewardship Economy: Chapter 14). These would include respect for existing property rights, no penalties for the poorest, no penalties for owners of low-value homes, ability to pay, fiscal neutrality and planning that reflects the collective will:

Respect for existing property rights

The stewardship fees for any site should be limited to any increase in its market rent that occurs after the onset of transition. This respects the full value of existing property rights, and even future expectations; according to rational expectations theory (see glossary) in orthodox economics these are understood to be priced in to current property values (Paul Samuelson & William Nordhaus 1992: 646).

No penalties for the poorest

There must be a guarantee that none of the poorest and most disadvantaged members of society will be worse off at any stage in the transition to stewardship.

No penalties for owners of low-value homes

For homes of below-average market rent, there needs to be a guarantee that homeowners are better-off under stewardship than ownership.

Ability to pay

The introduction of stewardship is intended to provide people with a financial incentive to make the best possible use of their land, or to pass it on to someone who will. This means that people who are living in homes that are of above average value, adjusted for the number of people living there (per capita market value), will feel a pressure to move to less valuable sites.

As people feel a strong attachment to their home, there need to be mechanisms during transition that enable them to stay in their own home – for example deferring payment of stewardship fees and rolling them up as a charge against their home until they sell it.

Fiscal neutrality

Government policy has been to try, albeit unsuccessfully, to maintain its income equal to its expenditure over the course of the economic cycle. Transition to stewardship should continue this same policy, ensuring that macroeconomic management of the economy continues as normal.

The ideal way to conform to this principle during transition to stewardship is to guarantee fiscal neutrality – that for every pound collected as stewardship fees a pound will be removed from existing taxes.

It would be tempting for government to introduce stewardship fees as an additional tax and use it, for example, to fund additional public services or to reduce the deficit or the national debt. For tactical reasons it is essential that this does not happen as stewardship fees would then be rightly described, and discredited, as a stealth tax.

This would undermine the credibility and acceptability of stewardship. If the government needs additional revenue it must raise this from other taxes and then replace these with stewardship fees so these can be seen to have the benefit of reducing conventional taxation.

There is a question whether strict fiscal neutrality would result in acceptable distributional consequences. Some of the revenue may be needed for a parallel reform of the benefit system with the introduction of a Universal Basic Income (Chapter 11).

Planning that reflects the collective will

Planning is at the heart of a stewardship economy and its reform would need to go along with transition. One immediately challenging issue is that stewardship cannot allow a steward unilaterally to place a restrictive covenant on their land as this reduces the stewardship fees they are liable to pay. During transition all existing covenants need to be reviewed and either ratified or rejected by the planning authority. Planning decisions should be the expression of the collective will.

Low but increasing levels of Land Value Tax and ten-year transition to stewardship

Most supporters of Land Value Taxation propose, when considering introducing it into an ownership economy, collecting a small but increasing percentage of the current market rent of land.

A ten year transition to stewardship

James Robertson

James Robertson has been one of the most consistent supporters of the proposal to tax land values and distribute a Universal Income. In a paper for the New Economics Foundation, he described an illustrative scenario for a 'ten-year switch' at the end of which land was to be taxed at 75 per cent of market rent (James Robertson 1994:33). He describes the year-by-year replacement of existing taxes and benefits that would need to take place over this time frame. The proposal advocated below appears to be less radical than James Robertson's as it proposes taxing only any increase in the market rent of land. However, if it were carried out during a time in which land prices are rising, such as the decade after his paper was published, the two proposals have a remarkably similar time course and impact.

Tony Vickers

Tony Vickers, in his book *Location Matters* (2007), describes a political timetable for transition to Land Value Taxation over the course of two parliaments, also a ten year transition. His proposal is sensitive to the real political and technical challenges and draws on many years of research on land taxes worldwide.

Advantages of low but increasing Land Value Tax

Starting with a low level of Land Value Tax and gradually building it up has several advantages, the most powerful of which is that a percentage of current market rent can be taxed without initially disturbing the traditional land market. Valuation of land can be carried out using the methods with which we are familiar, enhanced by the use of land value maps. The amount of tax can be set initially at a low enough level to be politically acceptable, and gradually increased over the years. And such an approach provides an immediate stream of income that will more than cover the cost of the initial valuation and set up of the tax mechanism.

Disadvantages of low but increasing Land Value Tax

From an ethical point of view this approach suffers from the serious disadvantage that a Land Value Tax levied on a proportion of the whole value of the land reduces its market value, and so fails to respect existing property rights. The pragmatic disadvantages are perhaps even more compelling. This sort of gradual transition to stewardship would be at risk from political reversal (Chapter 2).

Even if it proved possible to steadily increase the proportion of market rent collected as Land Value Tax, a point would be reached where the Land Value Tax caused significant falls in the market value of land. At this point the New Land Market would need to be introduced (Chapter 3), and the resistance would at that point be likely to be overwhelming.

Stewardship fees equal to increase in market rent

Stewardship economy: private property without private ownership advocates, as a mechanism for transition, levying fees of 100 per cent – not of market rent but of any increase in market rent that occurs after the scheme is introduced.

The ethical reason is that collecting 100 per cent of future increases in market rent appropriately manages the tension between the ethical arguments put forward in favour of stewardshipwith the need to fully respect existing property rights (Stewardship Economy: Chapter 14).

From a practical point of view, it would be best to introduce a New Land Market from the outset. This can be achieved by means of a small modification of the New Land Market during transition that grants to owners 100 per cent of the total value of their property (land as well as buildings) and collects only increases in the market rent of the land that occur after the onset of transition.

It is possible to imagine the collection of Land Value Taxes, equal to the increase in the market rent of land, as the first step in a long transition to a steady-state stewardship economy.

It is important to understand that taxing future increases in market rent is NOT in any way related to other sorts of land tax, in particular the Development Land Tax and its variants which may appear superficially similar. Development Land Tax is a tax that is applied in situations where an increase in the market value of land is revealed after development has actually takes place and is intended specifically for the purposes of Land Value Capture. Development Land Tax discourages development because landowners put developments on hold till the inevitable political reversal takes place. It generates only small amounts of revenue because it applies to only a tiny proportion of sites (Chapter 2). The arrangements for transition to stewardship, by contrast, ensure that there is nothing to be gained by delaying development once planning permission has been granted. They also make it possible to collect the increase in market rent from all land, no matter why the value has risen.

174

Advantages of taxing only the increase in market rent

The major advantage of this approach is that, once it is put into effect, the market value of land would immediately stop rising – even before a penny in tax was collected. The benefits that this immediately brings include abolishing land price booms (and busts) and eradicating speculation and speculative prices from the housing market.

In addition, there can then be no political haggling over how fast the transition should progress as this is determined entirely by how fast the market rent of land increases.

Disadvantages of taxing only the increase in market rent

One disadvantage is that this approach might produce little or no revenue in the early years, depending on the phase of the economic cycle at which it is introduced, and the set-up and valuation would then require seed funding.

More significantly, this sort of transition is only possible if market rents rise in the future. There are cyclical changes that may see falls in the market value of land, and in the long term the assumption that the market value of land will increase may be unrealistic in the light of the economic changes that will accompany climate change, prolonged recession and political instability.

Legal issues

Most states provide constitutional protection against confiscation of legally held property through a 'right to property'. This right doesn't prevent the state from imposing taxes on income from that property or indeed taxes amounting to a proportion of the total value of the property (in the case of Inheritance Tax). It does not prevent the state from collecting Council Tax, nor a tax based on property values, nor a Land Value Tax set at say 20 per cent of annual market rent. Legal protection would surely be invoked, quite rightly, if it were proposed to move instantly to a stewardship economy in which 100 per cent of the market rent was collected as stewardship fees.

It will be necessary to explore and avoid any potential legal barriers to transition in which only future increases in the market rent of the land are taxed.

Mortgages

One of the objections that is raised to the gradual introduction of stewardship fees is that mortgage lenders as well as owners of land would suffer from a fall in the market value of properties, reducing the value of the collateral they hold on their loans and potentially threatening the stability of the banking system. The trajectory for transition to stewardship described here does not suffer from this problem. There is no confiscation of property rights, the market value of the steward's assets are preserved and the lender's collateral along with it.

A practical proposal for transition

Initial property valuations

The practical proposal described above for a steady-state stewardship economy (Chapter 8) needs to be modified for transition from an ownership economy, so that stewardship fees amount only the rise in market value since the start of the transition. The Registered Improvement Value is the part of the property that the steward owns, and instead of setting this equal to the Depreciated Replacement Cost of the improvements alone it is set at the Market Value of the whole property at the onset of transition – the Transitional Value.

Registered Improvement Value

- The owner of each interest in each site estimates the market value of their property (improvements plus land). The Land Stewardship Trust verifies the valuation and adjusts it if necessary. This value is designated the 'Transitional Value' of that property.

- The initial valuation of the property at the onset of transition poses a significant challenge. The market value of land in an ownership economy is not simply a capitalisation of future expected rents. Purchasers usually buy with the expectation that their investment will rise in value, and this adds a speculative element to the price. Once people are convinced that stewardship is going to be introduced, this speculative element would disappear. It would be important to allow this fall in property prices to happen before the valuation is carried out. If not, in areas where there is a speculative element to land values the Registered Improvement Value would be set too high, and the stewardship fees (which, during transition, are based on increase in market rent) too low.

- The Registered Improvement Value is set equal to this Transitional Value (not to the Depreciated Replacement Cost of the building).

- This means that the steward owns the improvements plus the full market value of the land. If the property were to change hands by auction at this time the stewardship fees would be zero.

- When the property changes hands at a later date it will be transferred to whoever bids the highest stewardship fees in addition to paying the Registered Improvement Value to the outgoing steward.

Stewardship fees

It is not in the public interest to subsidise property owners when the value of their land has fallen, so if there are no positive bids for the stewardship fees these are set to zero and the property is sold to whoever is prepared to pay the highest Improvement Value. This amount becomes the Registered Improvement Value.

In this way stewardship fees become payable as and when the market rent of land rises over the course of time.

Appeal

If an owner cannot agree with the Land Stewardship Trust and thinks that the Transitional Value of the property is worth more, they can appeal to the market. The Land Stewardship Trust would conduct an auction, but this would be an auction of the market value of the whole property (the value of land plus improvements) not an auction for the stewardship fees. In view of the Revenue Equivalence Theorem this would probably be conducted as a second-price auction (Chapter 7). Potentially collusive bids to drive up the market value would be forbidden; for example, from the owner, their family members or companies of which they are a director.

This is not an ideal arrangement and remains open to corruption, but it has to be provided only once for each property, at the onset of transition.

Registered Improvement Values during transition

There are then several possible options for how to treat the Registered Improvement Value in subsequent years.

One approach would be to fix the Registered Improvement Value at a constant level in nominal (money) terms. Inflation would then erode the real value of the original owner's property. This may seem unfair to the landowner if they think of their property as an investment; but if they come to regard it as a consumption good this may be acceptable. Most of us would be quite happy if we could sell our old car for the same amount of money that we paid for it when it was new.

Another approach would be to index the Registered Improvement Value at the rate of inflation. In this case the owner would retain the full value of their property indefinitely. The problem with this is that it is the value of their land as well as their improvements that is being indexed. The benefits of existing land ownership would be preserved indefinitely.

A preferable approach would probably be to index the Registered Improvement Value but at a level that is below the annual rate of inflation.

Indexing the Registered Improvement Value at some proportion of the rate of inflation would ensure that a homeowner would see the value of their home increasing in nominal terms even though it was falling in real terms.

Since about half the value of most homes is currently the value of the land and half the value of the buildings, indexing at 50 per cent of the rate of inflation would be roughly equivalent to indexing the value of the buildings fully but the land not at all. The stewardship fees then reflect the real increase in market rent of the land that occurs after the onset of transition even though the basis of valuation is not the increase in market rent but half the increase in the rental of the whole property.

As the Registered Improvement Value rises at below the rate of inflation while the Replacement Cost (and so in most cases the Depreciated Replacement Cost) of the building rises at the rate of inflation the Registered Improvement Value will eventually fall to equal the Depreciated Replacement Cost.

At this point the Registered Improvement Value could be abandoned and the owner would own the Depreciated Replacement Cost of the building as in a fully established stewardship economy.

Special Cases

There will be cases that need special handling during transition. The challenge is to find ways of doing so that do not contravene the principles of stewardship or undermine the likelihood of complete transition. Examples of such cases include land owned by charities and Community Land Trusts.

Charities

As land values rise after the onset of transition, charities start to pay stewardship fees. The benefits they derive from the removal of existing taxes will be less than those derived by other businesses, as they are currently exempt from a number of taxes (80 per cent to 100 per cent relief on Business Rates as well as tax reliefs on donations, profits from trading that relates to their primary purpose, rental and investment income, acquisition and disposal of property and some categories of VAT).

As they lose this indirect subsidy that they receive in ownership economies, they are at risk of losing their competitive advantage over non-charity businesses.

The temptation is to exempt charities from having to pay stewardship fees, but this is absolutely to be avoided as it would introduce massive distortions into the economy and the behaviour of charities (Stewardship Economy: Chapter 8).

It would be possible to identify the extent of the loss of subsidy and for the government to set aside some appropriate amount as a direct subsidy. The Charity Commissioners would then become responsible for deciding how best to make use of this to support charities.

Community Land Trusts

Community Land Trusts would need to be treated as a special case during transition from ownership to stewardship. Consider the position of an established Community Land Trust at the time when transition to stewardship begins. A member's Registered Improvement Value is equal to the Depreciated Replacement Cost of the building as they own their home but not the land. The Community Land Trust becomes the steward of the land that it holds in trust and becomes liable to pay the stewardship fees (equal to the market rent), which imposes additional costs on the Trust.

Suppose that the Community Land Trust is exposed to paying the full market rent for the land while receiving only a lower level of rent from its property-holders. The Community Land Trust would have to decide, and to be allowed to decide, what to do: to charge the property holder enough rent to pay the stewardship fees that it now incurs; to charge the existing rent and find other ways to subsidise the property holder; or to sell their interest to a new steward for the Transitional Value of the land on the open market. In this case the low-rent possibilities of the site disappears, apart from any subsidy provided by the

Community Land Trust, and the rest of society benefits from the stewardship fees paid.

This impact could be avoided if planning restrictions were placed on the land, stipulating that this land can only be used to provide housing at zero rent for the land. In this case its market rent is zero, the Transitional Value of the land is zero and the Transitional Value of the whole property is equal to the Depreciated Replacement Cost. Here the members and Community Land Trust remain undisturbed, and the rest of society receives no stewardship fees from that land.

When to start the transition

Even in simple systems, the impact of change depends on timing. Push a pendulum when it is travelling one way and you increase its swing, push in the same direction when it is at a different stage in its travel, and you stop it. Increase interest rates one day and it takes the edge off inflation, increase them by the same amount six months later and it triggers a recession. In complex systems where the link between cause and effect is uncertain it is only possible to think of interventions as disturbances or perturbations that may, or may not, disturb the system so that it moves from one set of configurations (basin of attraction) to another.

One thing that is well worth trying to predict, though, is when would be the most likely time for transition to be acceptable. Homeowners have short memories (less than 18 years (Stewardship Economy: Ch 8), anyway) and during the upswing of the economic cycle they behave as though their home will continue to rise in value for ever. This is not a time when there will be any popular support for transition to stewardship. But after the peak has passed and house prices have stagnated or fallen, perhaps leaving some people with negative equity, the idea is more appealing. When this memory is fresh, but land prices are beginning to rise again, there may be one of those windows of opportunity when there is political will to embark on a transition to stewardship, at least in a pilot site.

How fast to make the transition

Taking the approach to transition described above, the pace of transition cannot be determined or controlled, but is driven entirely by the behaviour of the economy. If land values rise rapidly the transition occurs rapidly; if they stagnate the transition pauses till they begin to rise again. This is a safe and natural way to make change, though it may increase the risks of political reversal.

It's interesting to compare this with James Robertson's illustrative scenario. At the end of his three-year lead-in to 1996 followed by a ten-year transition to 2007, 75 per cent of the market rent of land would have been collected as Land Value Tax.

What actually happened over these ten years to 2007 was that the market rent and market value of homes increased approximately threefold so two thirds of their value in 2007 had been added during the previous ten years. Even if the buildings had increased in value by as much as the land this would mean that the increase in the market rent of land since 1997 was equal to 66 per cent of its market rent in 2007; as almost all of the increase in value was in the land, the increase in the market rent of the land will have been about 75 per cent of its market rent in 2007. If stewardship had been introduced in 1997, stewardship fees would in 2007 have been equal to at least 75 per cent of the market rent – exactly the same level that James Robertson proposed but by a different route.

This gives an indication of the speed at which stewardship could be introduced. In a booming economy as much as 75 per cent of the transition could take place over 15 years, and even in a slowly growing economy this would be likely to take 20 to 25 years. If it were introduced at times of house price stagnation it would take far longer – which would be entirely appropriate.

The initial benefit of declaring the start of transition is that, provided there was political credibility that it would not be reversed, the market value of land would be expected never to rise above its value at the start of transition. Stewardship discourages the holding of land unless it is being put to its highest and best use, so at the onset of transition a great deal of currently underused land – empty and second homes, unproductive land banks, derelict industrial sites – would either be put to use or put on the market. The first order effect of this increase in supply of land would be to reduce the market rent and market value of land generally, so during this period of time stewardship fees would be zero on most land. As this influx of land stimulated the economy, however, the demand for land and so its market rent would begin to rise, and eventually exceed its market rent at the onset of transition, at which point stewardship fees would start to be paid.

Summary: This chapter has described a practical approach by which any increase in the market rent of land that occurs after the onset of transition can be measured and collected.

The steward retains the value that the whole property, land plus buildings, had at the onset of transition – at least in nominal terms.

If the Registered Improvement Value of the property is indexed by less than the rate of inflation its value will eventually fall below the Depreciated Replacement Cost of the building and the steward can then choose to have the value of their improvements set equal to the Depreciated Replacement Cost.

The rate of transition depends fundamentally on the rate of economic growth, which is the main determinant of the rate of increase in land values. Transition would probably be at least 50 per cent complete within 25 years of the start of transition.

Particular care needs to be taken with charities and Community Land Trusts, which have benefited from special treatment in ownership economies.

As well as the collection of stewardship fees, the other aspect of a stewardship economy that needs consideration is how to make best use of the revenue that it raises (Chapter 11).

Chapter 12 Spending the revenue

In an *established* stewardship economy, the revenue from stewardship fees would be used as a source of government revenue and the remainder to fund a Universal Income.

Transition from ownership to stewardship is complicated, not because stewardship is complicated but because the current system of taxes and benefits has to be unravelled in a way that it disadvantages as few people as possible, particularly the least well off.

As revenue becomes available, it could be used in several ways (Stewardship Economy 2011:129):

- to allow the removal of conventional taxes

- to introduce a Universal Income in addition to the existing benefit system

- to introduce a Universal Income as an alternative to a set of existing benefits

- provide a Universal Income that is subject to Income Tax and partial withdrawal of existing benefits.

The revenue from stewardship fees should not be used as an additional source of government revenue, or it will become discredited as a stealth tax.

This chapter begins by discussing some general principles including the importance of exploring and modelling the impact on a range of different people. It then discusses the replacement of conventional taxes which would boost the economy as a whole by removing their deadweight loss. This would lead to a virtuous circle of rising land values, rising stewardship fees and further tax replacement. It discusses how to introduce a Universal Income, and the choices that could be made about the balance between Universal Income and replacement of taxes, each of which has a different distributional effect. It goes on to provide a thought experiment where there is an immediate switch to a stewardship economy (rather than the gradual transition proposed). There is more about Universal Income in book 4.

General principles

The principles for transition to the payment of stewardship fees are set out above (Chapter 11). A fair transition requires a carefully designed use of the revenue which is likely to include a mix of tax substitution and Universal Income. In practice this can only be achieved if the consequences for different sorts of household are modelled thoroughly enough to ensure that it always benefits the poorest members of society. In a real transition the gradual introduction of stewardship fees equal to the increase in market rent would reveal the amount of revenue available at every stage.

Any proposals for transition should be subjected to rigorous modelling of the likely consequences, particularly for the distribution of income and wealth, the poorest members of society, the economy as a whole and for its regional impact – for example using a microsimulation model such as EUROMOD.

An essential principle of transition from ownership to stewardship is that stewardship fees should be introduced not as a tax (a source of government revenue) which would be described as a stealth tax but as a charge or fees for the use of land. This means that, during transition, the government should use the revenue to reduce and replace existing taxes or distribute it as a Universal Income. If the government wants to fund additional spending or to reduce the deficit or national debt, they should raise other taxes for this purpose (Stewardship Economy: Chapter 14).

Using the revenue from stewardship fees to reduce existing taxes is fiscally neutral and can be carried out in a way that is transparent. It has the great economic advantage of stimulating the economy by removing the deadweight loss of conventional taxes. It broadly counterbalances the expenditure on stewardship fees by property owners.

Removing orthodox taxes

The impact of tax replacement on market rents

Suppose that stewardship fees were to be introduced overnight while maintaining current taxes and benefits (this is a thought experiment not a policy proposal). The total stewardship fees received would be equal to the total current market rent. Demand for land for speculation would fall and supply would increase as investors and holders of under-used land released it. As the market rent of land fell, those who are currently unable to afford land would enter the market.

Then suppose (again as a thought experiment) that this revenue from stewardship fees replaced conventional taxes (leaving the benefit system unchanged). All taxpayers would see their disposable incomes rise, though not enough to fully compensate all current landowners, particularly those with large and valuable landholdings.

It is likely that most people would use most of their increase in income to continue to compete for access to land because it is essential for living and working. This would cause market rents to rise, and stewardship fees would rise along with them. This in turn would provide additional revenue from stewardship fees that could be used to fund further tax cuts. If the demand for land holds up then tax cuts lead to a more-or-less equal (100 per cent) increase in stewardship fees. This self-reinforcing (positive) feedback loop then creates a virtuous tax-replacement cycle that comes to an end only when there are no more taxes that the government wants to reduce or remove.

After these changes had been put into effect, the total level of stewardship fees would be more or less equal to the sum of the total market rent of the UK before the tax reductions began plus an amount equal to the taxes removed (which would provide the government with the same revenue that it used to receive from conventional taxation).

As an illustration: The total tax take for the UK in 2007-8 was £416 billion, excluding taxes on oil, tobacco and alcohol which would be likely to be retained in a stewardship economy. In addition, Council Tax amounted to just over £20 billion England, equivalent to about £34 billion for the UK, giving a total tax take of about £450 billion.

UK Revenue 2007-8	£bn
Income tax (net of tax credits)	155.1
NIC	98.2
VAT	84.9
Corporation Tax (net of tax credits)	46.8
Stamp Duty Land Tax	13.7
Other	17.5
Total HMRC	416.2
Council Tax	34.0
TOTAL	450.2

UK total tax take 2007-8

While there is no reliable estimate availabile for the current total market rent of the land in the UK, Ronald Banks and colleagues estimated the value of land in Great Britain in 1985 and, from this, converted market values to market rent (1989). I have adjusted these market rents to January 2009 usng the Department of Communities and Local Government index for house prices. (See Chapter 5 for more detail about methods for estimating market rent of the UK.)

	With current taxes £bn Market rent	With taxes removed £bn Market rent
Public service	19	
Farm & woodland	14	45
Housing	119	372
Commerce	51	161
Industry	26	83
TOTAL excluding public land	211	661

Estimated market rents 2009

If these taxes were removed, market rents would be likely to rise to around £660 billion (£211 billion existing market rent plus £450 billion increase in market rent as taxes are withdrawn). (See Stewardship Economy book 7 for explanation of deadweight loss)

Most of this £660 billion comes from housing, commerce and industry with less than 7 per cent arising from farm and woodland. These figures are very approximate, but we need them only to give an idea of where we might get to rather than for planning purposes. Transition could be safely conducted by using the stewardship fees that are actually collected to fund exactly equal tax cuts, rather than basing tax cuts on projections.

Retained taxes

Some taxes may be retained in a stewardship economy in order to influence behaviour or redistribute wealth. Taxes on alcohol and tobacco are likely to be retained, along with environmental taxes and charges.

Some versions of transition to a stewardship economy might also delay the removal of income tax until pay differentials had fallen to more reasonable levels than at present, and Inheritance Tax might be retained to combat the disadvantages experienced by the poor across the generations.

The decision about which taxes to retain is, of course, a political one. Retained taxes will not generate additional revenue, as they reduce people's disposable income and cause a corresponding reduction market rents and so in stewardship fees.

Inflation

If the rising stewardship fees are included in the basket of prices that are used to measure inflation, the transition will be judged to be inflationary. If they are not included, just as housing costs are not included in the Consumer Price Index, transition to stewardship of land will not be inflationary.

It will be important at this stage not to adjust monetary and fiscal policy in response to these changes, and in particular not to respond to increases in inflation if these are caused by the use of an inflation measure that includes the increase in market rent.

Introducing Universal Income

Instead of, or as well as, using the revenue from stewardship fees to reduce taxes, it could be used to fund a Universal Income – either in addition to existing benefits or as an alternative to some existing benefits.

It is possible to estimate the level of Universal Income that could be paid in an established steady-state stewardship economy if the whole of the current market rent of the country were to be used for that purpose. Universal Income could be paid at a modest level in addition to existing benefits or at a higher level as an alternative to a bundle of 'replaced benefits'. Transition could follow a course towards either of these; or towards a hybrid that is partly additional and partly an alternative to existing benefits.

In addition to existing benefits

It is in principle straightforward to introduce stewardship into a low-consumption economy where there is little in the way of a benefit system.

If Universal Income were to be introduced in addition to the extensive system of benefits found in most high-consumption economies the advantage is that it would benefit everyone, including the poorest, from the very start without disrupting the current benefit system. One disadvantage of this approach is that it offers no opportunity, even in the long run, of reforming the existing conditional benefit system with all of its disadvantages including means-testing and the unemployment trap. Another is the low level of Universal Income that it would provide.

As an alternative to existing benefits

The challenge of introducing a Universal Income as an alternative to a set of existing benefits arises from the complexity of a mature ownership economy. Some benefits, such as benefits paid to people with disabilities and with caring responsibilities, would be retained in any liberal or socialist version of a stewardship economy. There would be a choice about whether others, such as sickness benefit, are retained or replaced by a Universal Income. Universal Income would replace benefits that are already close to being universal for a particular age group, such as Child Benefit and Basic State Pension, along with benefits and tax credits that are conditional on low income and unemployment.

Universal Income introduced as an alternative to existing benefits for those on low income or unemployed offers the prospect of raising people out of dependence on benefits. However, if these benefits and tax credits are withdrawn pound for pound as the Universal Income is introduced, those dependent on these benefits would not gain from the reform.

As a hybrid

There is therefore a trade-off between providing an immediate improvement for the poorest by introducing Universal Income in addition to benefits and reforming the benefit system by introducing Universal Income as an alternative. Universal Income may be introduced in a whole range of hybrids between the extremes of addition and alternative, with the intent of combining the benefits of both.

For example, the Universal Income could be introduced in addition to existing benefits, so everyone receives it from the start, while subjecting it during transition to income tax. It should be noted that this taxation contravenes a basic principle of a Citizens' Income funded from general taxation, which is that it is non-withdrawable. Taxation is proposed only as a temporary measure during transition, so in an established stewardship economy the Universal Income would meet all the criteria for a Citizen's Income.

Taxpayers would remit 20 to 40 per cent of their Universal Income for as long as income tax remained in force, say an average of 25 per cent. And households on benefit would have some of their traditional benefits withdrawn that could be set at 25 per cent of the Universal Income that they receive.

If the Universal Income is introduced gradually up to three times the level of 'replaced' benefits then the deductions from traditional benefits will be equal to the original level of these benefits and they can be completely withdrawn. By this stage the Universal Income, net of tax or withdrawal of benefits, is three times the original level of these benefits.

Tax replacement combined with Universal Income

So far, this chapter has considered how to use the revenue from stewardship fees, either to replace taxes or to fund a Universal Income. Each approach has its advantages, and in practice there would be a strong case for using some of the revenue for each of these purposes. One example worth modelling would include:

- full retention of benefits for people with disabilities and people with caring responsibilities

- revenue from land used for non-domestic purposes (commercial, industrial, retail and agricultural) used to replace taxes on business (Chapter 15)

- the revenue from residential land used initially to replace a reformed Council Tax, and then a hybrid Universal Income (Chapter 15)

Universal Income treated as taxable income until

- income tax is removed

- for every £1 per week of Universal Income a person's existing benefit package reduced by around 30p per week.

The changes to non-domestic land would boost the economy and the changes to domestic land would begin the reform of the benefit system. It would bear heavily on owner-occupiers who use their land inefficiently (particularly single people with high-value properties).

The opportunities and some of the apparent complexity are caused not by stewardship itself, which is a very simple and straightforward proposal, but by the need to unravel the complexities of the dysfunctional traditional tax-benefit system.Thought experiment: 100% of market rent collected and used for Universal Income

This section describes a thought experiment in which stewardship fees equal to 100 per cent of the market rent of land are introduced overnight, and all the revenue used to introduce a Universal Income. It considers three scenarios:

- the collection of stewardship fees replaces all existing taxes and Universal Income is paid in addition to existing benefits

- the collection of stewardship fees replaces all existing taxes and Universal Income replaces existing benefits

- Universal Income is subject to income tax and there is partial withdrawal of benefits.

The revenue from stewardship fees, at 2009 prices and taxes, is assumed to be about £180 billion (chapter 5).

Stewardship fees replace all existing taxes

This thought experiment takes place in the UK with its existing system of taxes and benefits. None of these are realistic propositions for transition, but each provides interesting insights that contribute to imagining the sorts of transition that might be worth modelling.

Imagine that stewardship was introduced overnight, and stewardship fees introduced equal to £180 billion. The immediate impact would be the removal of £180 billion in existing taxes. This would result in a rise in people's disposable income, allowing them to compete more fiercely for existing land. Market rents of land, and so stewardship fees, would rise. The government could then use this further revenue to reduce other taxes, leading to a virtuous cycle in which taxes are eliminated (at least those that we want to eliminate) and the market rents of land rise.

In addition, if the deadweight loss of, say, half of all existing taxation was removed, this would lead to an increase in GDP of perhaps 15 per cent, leading to further rises in the market rent of land and so in government revenue.

Universal Income in addition to existing benefits

In the 'addition scenario' all existing benefits are retained and the Universal Income is paid in addition to these. The Universal Income could be an equal payment for each person, or it could be age-related. The logic of stewardship suggests that the Universal Income should be distributed on an equal basis no matter what the recipient's age. If the available revenue were to be distributed in equal shares to all the 61 million inhabitants of the UK, each person would receive an additional income of about £3,000 per year (£2,950 per year or £56.74 per week). If the Universal Income were to be age-related, the £180 billion revenue could provide a Universal Income, in addition to existing benefits, at the levels shown below (Column 5 in table on next page). These levels are about two thirds of the amount the current benefit system considers to be adequate for survival – the maximum level of benefit available in an ownership economy (Child

Benefit + Child Tax Credit, Income Support or Pension Credit, depending on age).

	UK population			Cost of UI		
	thousands	thousands	millions			
age	M	F	Total	UI pp pw	UI pp pa	Total cost (bn)
up to 1	404	385	1	£56	£2,922	£2
1 to 17	6,319	6,013	12	£49	£2,556	£32
18-24	2,998	2,851	6	£43	£2,239	£13
25-59	14,332	14,513	29	£43	£2,239	£65
60-64	1,778	1,861	4	£87	£4,527	£16
65+	4,321	5,609	10	£101	£5,237	£52
Total	30,151	31,232	61			£180

Who benefits from Universal Income as an addition?

Immediate impact

Introducing Universal Income as an addition to existing benefits and tax credits in a stewardship economy means that everyone benefits immediately that the first payments are made, including the poorest people currently receiving the highest levels of benefit.

In the simplest case of an age-independent Universal Income, every man, woman and child benefits from a private income of about £3,000 per year. The immediate impact of introducing stewardship fees at 100 per cent of market rent combined with a Universal Income will have different impacts on each household, but there are broad differences between tenants, landlords and owner-occupiers.

Tenants are not liable to pay stewardship fees. Unless the income of tenants increases or the landlord had set the rent at below market rates, landlords cannot pass their stewardship fees on to their tenants through increase in rent because an immediate rise in rent would force a tenant out and a landlord would forfeit their income. So, the short term impact on tenants is that each person benefits by the full amount of the Universal Income, about £3,000 per year. This is, however, only the immediate impact. See below.

Most landlords also own their own home. They can be considered to be both landlord and owner-occupier, and their Universal Income taken into account in relation to their owner-occupation. Landlords pay stewardship fees, and assuming that about half the market rent of each property is the market rent of the land (the other half that of the buildings and other improvements), the immediate impact is that they lose about half their previous income. This, as with tenants, is the immediate impact.

Consider a single person who is an owner-occupier of a modest home that has a market rent of about £6,000 per year (£3,000 per year for the market rent of the land assuming that half the value is in the land and half is in the building). They will receive as much in Universal Income as they pay out in stewardship fees. A couple will receive twice as much, and f they have two children they will receive £12,000 per year.

Introduction Cycle

The increase in the disposable incomes of tenants will lead to a cycle in which the market rent of their homes increases and the stewardship fees paid by the landlord increase, the costs of which are, in due course, passed on to the tenant. If the rent that they pay is a market rent, tenants, as a whole, will be in the same position as at the outset. This assumes that each dwelling is uniquely suited to a family of a particular size, and that Housing Benefit does not rise to take account of the increase in market rents. If the rent the tenant pays is controlled, they will continue to benefit from the increase in their disposable income.

Landlords charging market rents for their properties will find that these rise as the incomes of their tenants increase. This will be approximately enough to pay the stewardship fees unless tenants' rents are controlled.

Some relatively low-value homes will increase in market rent and market value as their owner-occupiers receive an increase in disposable income and new purchasers push up the price. This increase in market value will further increase the stewardship fees due, and this will put a limit on the increase in the market values.

The market rent and market value of most owner-occupied homes will fall as new purchasers have lower disposable incomes and are unable to offer as much as they had been before the introduction of stewardship fees and the Universal Income. Stewardship fees will fall, and this will put a limit on the fall in market values.

Across the whole housing market, prices will converge somewhat with the prices of high-value homes falling and the prices of low-value homes rising.

However, the major disadvantage of introducing Universal Income in addition to existing taxes and benefits is that does not make it easier for people to take on part-time and low paid work. It does nothing to replace taxes with the deadweight loss that they impose on the economy.

Universal Income as an alternative to existing benefits

It would be possible to imagine introducing the Universal Income and withdrawing existing benefits on a pound-for-pound basis. In this scenario people's total income from Universal Income and residual benefits would be unchanged. It would seem unfair that the poorest members of society, those on benefits, do not benefit from the introduction of the Universal Income. Those of them who do not own land would, on the other hand, be paying none of the stewardship fees. But benefit recipients who own land (and there are many recipients of the

Basic State Pension in this category) would be hard hit by the need to pay stewardship fees while receiving no net benefit from Universal Income.

The big advantage of introducing Universal Income as an alternative to existing benefits is that people whose benefits were, in an ownership economy, conditional on unemployment or poverty now receive an unconditional income. They can work and earn with all the benefits this brings to them individually and to the economy as a whole.

The disadvantage is that this has some distributional effects that are not ideal. The position of a landlord is the same during the introduction cycle as when the Universal Income is introduced as an addition to existing benefits, although there may be a difference following that time. Tenants benefit 20 to 40 per cent less from the 'alternative' reform scenario than they would from the 'addition' scenario, unless they are amongst the group who are not currently eligible for benefits but also earn too little to pay tax. In this case they benefit from the full Universal Income.

Owner-occupiers, like tenants, benefit less from this scenario unless they too do not receive benefits and their income is too low to incur tax. Homeowners with above-average value homes will be disadvantaged by introducing Universal Income as an alternative to existing benefits, as will many single people throughout the country, even in a home whose value is below the local average and many couples throughout the country living in a home whose value is above the local average couples in the south living in a home whose value is above the local average.

Single owner-occupiers who are currently eligible to receive means-tested benefits will be likely be disadvantaged.

Universal Income subject to income tax and partial withdrawal of benefits

This scenario is intended to illustrate a half-way house between introducing the Universal Income as an addition to existing benefits and introducing it as an alternative. Here the Universal Income is introduced with the intention of ultimately replacing most benefits (other than for disability, carers, maternity and perhaps sickness) with the Universal Income. The underlying principle would be that nobody suffered a reduction in their overall income as the result of this reform.

One way of achieving this would be for some percentage, say 40 per cent, of each person's Universal Income to be deducted from the benefit package of their household. To take as an example a family of two adults and two children, receiving a new total income of £12,000 per year from their Universal Income, £4,800 per year would be deducted from their existing package of benefits. This would still leave them £7,200 per year better off than they had been. The £4,800 per year that the government recovers, either in reduced benefits or in Income Tax, could be used to increase the level of Universal Income.

Mitigation during transition

In a long-established stewardship economy, one that had been in place for generations, people would be accustomed to saving for their old age and to moving to smaller homes as their income fell on retirement. The housing provided would allow this to happen easily, with many more mixed developments suitable for people at all stages of life.

During transition to stewardship, people would face difficult choices. Households on higher incomes would have to decide whether to pay the stewardship fee for their home or to move to a less expensive home. It will be important not to put people under undue pressure to leave their family home. If they decide to stay, it would be important to allow them to be able to draw down the capital tied up in the building that they own to pay their stewardship fee.

But during the transition to stewardship even the hybrid scenario has the disadvantage that it penalises certain people, including those who live alone, or are asset-rich and income-poor or receive means-tested benefits like pension credit. These impacts would be mitigated by the gradual transition to stewardship, an extension of Housing Benefit to owner-occupiers and the ability to choose between traditional benefits and the Universal Income.

The proposed transition is very different from the thought experiment described above. Stewardship fees are set not at the market rent of the land but at the increase in the market rent of the land that has occurred since the onset of transition. This gives time for people to react to the coming changes.

Owner-occupiers are not currently eligible for Housing Benefit as they do not pay rent. During transition only, eligibility for Housing Benefit may need to be extended to these owner-occupiers for the limited purpose of enabling them to pay their stewardship fees (not their whole housing costs) for an appropriate category of dwelling.

During transition, each household must have the option of choosing whether all its members receive the Universal Income or whether the household receives its existing benefits. It will be important to ensure that the value of these existing benefits is not eroded. They need to be indexed year on year (in line with earnings not prices). And benefits that are currently conditional on payment of National Insurance Contributions need to be retained even after these contributions have been phased out.

This would provide a clear guarantee that no one would be worse-off, and households would be free to choose how they are supported. Different households will find it beneficial to transfer to Universal Income at different stages, with those on the lowest levels of benefit transferring earlier than those on higher levels.

Next steps – a microsimulation exercise

This chapter has provided a limited illustration of how the revenue from stewardship fees could be used, and some sense of the challenges.

Any serious proposal to introduce stewardship fees would need to be very thoroughly explored by modelling its consequences for a wide variety of different sorts of households. The 'back of the envelope' calculations in this chapter suggest that a fair and effective proposal will be likely to consist of some combination of the removal of orthodox taxes and the introduction of a Universal Income that is accompanied by both a partial withdrawal of existing benefits and is subject to Income Tax while this remains.

EUROMOD is a public domain microsimulation model of the UK (and other EU) tax-benefit systems. It was developed to explore the impact of changes in the tax-benefit system on households of different types. It will be necessary to use this, or similar, model, to identify the gains and losses of different sorts of household in order to fine-tune the design of transition.

Chapter 15 takes these insights and develops them into an approach in three parallel streams – in which domestic land, non-domestic land and the environment are treated independently and in a timescale that is appropriate.

Chapter 13 Transition where land reform is desired

One of the situations that could trigger the introduction of stewardship is a situation where there is political support for land reform, for example where there are no existing titles or claims to land (Chapter 9). Stewardship could provide a way to achieve the aims of land reform at low cost and without the risk of violence.

The need for land reform

In most high-consumption countries the pattern of land ownership is securely established. There may, however, be appetite for land reform where land holdings are spectacularly unequal and relationships still have feudal features, including the Highlands and Islands of Scotland, or where there are substantial numbers of absentee, and particularly foreign, landlords, for example, in Estonia and perhaps even London.

Land reform appears more often on the agenda of lower-consumption economies. In countries with a history of communism this was because land was held by the state for almost a century, and at the time of transition to capitalism there were real questions about how best to allocate the land. Land reform may also be desired in countries with a history of colonialism, either because this period of history has not left them with a system of recording legal title to land or because it has left them with a seriously inequitable distribution of land ownership.

Ownership economy

In an ownership economy the first step of a land reform programme is for the state is to acquire the land that is to be redistributed. This may be by coercion, either legal or illegal; or by purchase, which may be compulsory or voluntary.

Purchase is expensive, and the cost will limit the extent and the pace of land reform. Coercion, even if apparently successful in the short term, stores up problems for the future and leaves the way open to further rounds of coercive land transfers.

Once land has been acquired, the next step is to identify the beneficiaries of the land reform. There is a risk that the land is redistributed to the supporters of the government. And even when the land has been redistributed the long-term problem remains – how to ensure fair and equal access to land into the future, particularly as the population grows.

Stewardship economy

A stewardship economy provides an alternative to one-off land reform. Its introduction produces an economy in which those who can make best use of the land do so, and they compensate everyone else. Land reform is achieved by rapid transition to stewardship, during which landowners who are making little use of land (which may include the government) release their land as the result of economic self-interest, while those who believe they can make more efficient use of it bid to pay what they can afford. Everyone benefits from a Universal Income, and this allows everyone to become a steward of at least a fair share of the land if they want to do so.

In this way land reform becomes not a series of revolutionary changes but a continuous process of re-allocation of land to whoever chooses to compensate others for their use of it.

It is important to be aware of dangers in this approach for indigenous peoples, who may be drawn in to the global money economy with all the damage that can do. They should always be given the choice of opting out of the whole apparatus of stewardship.

Transition from state ownership

Eastern Europe

In Eastern Europe a great deal of land had been confiscated by the Nazis and this was taken over and collectivised by communist governments after 1945. Land rights became a major source of wealth and power in command and control economies, as they can be allocated to reward compliant behaviour or act as currency for favours and bribes.

Many Eastern European countries passed laws to return property to its original owners, though the impact varied considerably from country to country. This may have been well-intentioned but provided considerable scope for corruption.

If the states of Eastern Europe had swiftly introduced Land Value Taxation they could have avoided economic failure and could indeed have led the rest of the world in economic growth and development. Even the first step, producing an up to date and publicly accessible register of land and natural resources, would, however, have threatened the vested interests of the powerful and prevented their wholesale capture of resource rents.

Mikhail Gorbachev, as president of the USSR, initiated glasnost (openness) and perestroika (restructuring of the economy to allow private ownership of business and so the transition from command to market economy. He always believed that private ownership of artefacts (the things that we make) as well as secure use-rights to the land should be complemented with the payment of rent to the state for this land (Noyes 1991:4).

There was substantial interest in Land Value Taxation in Russia around 1991, supported by geoclassical economists from the West, but the advice from orthodox neoclassical economists in the West and pressure from the International Monetary Fund promoted the Washington Consensus, including private ownership rights to land and natural resources, and privatisation of state assets (Fred Harrison 2008:27). Private ownership of land and natural resources was finally written in to Russia's new constitution by Boris Yeltsin (Fred Harrison 2016:27). Ownership of state assets was contested and in the mid-1990s a small number of oligarchs, many of whom were relatives and associates of government officials, captured the resource rents of Russia's natural assets –particularly oil and gas.

China

Rural land in China was confiscated and transferred into collective ownership by Mao Tse-Tung during the Great Leap Forward. More recently peasants have been granted 30 year leases to farmland, but these leases do not allow farmers to sell up and move, to consolidate holdings or to use the land as collateral for loans to improve the land. This form of tenure is not even secure as swathes of countryside continue to be appropriated without compensation for industry and housing, particularly close to cities. In the villages, title to much of the land is unclear and unenforceable. Land disputes are a major cause of social unrest in both rural and urban areas.

Urban land is state-owned and held on leases of 40-70 years. There has been widespread privatisation of urban housing in China over the last decade, and the middle classes are anxious to ensure that these assets are safe from appropriation by the state. China enshrined private property rights in its constitution in 2004, and legislation in 2007 provides protection for the ownership of assets. There is serious opposition from those who see this as both a betrayal of the country's socialist principles and a reward for officials who used the privatisation process for personal gain (Economist 2007 (a):25).

Two of China's economic problems are house price bubbles and local authority finances. Local authorities raise revenue by compulsorily purchasing rural land, compensating farmers for the agricultural value of the land, and selling it to developers at its development value. This causes widespread protests as the farmers feel they are cheated out of the value of their land, and at the same time fails to provide anything more than one-off gains for the state (Economist 2012: 54).

Stewardship would provide security of tenure for all landholdings while at the same time ensuring that everyone receives an equal share of the market rent of the entire country. It would stabilise land prices and provide a regular stream of government revenue.

The challenges of setting up a comprehensive database of land ownership and providing a mechanism for distributing a

Universal Income would be considerable. There would also be likely to be significant political opposition from the urban property-owning class. Stewardship might, however, face fewer challenges in a setting in which land has been state-owned within living memory and in which there is significant opposition to private ownership of land. Transition would also be simpler and speedier than in a high-consumption economy with a comprehensive benefits system.

Cambodia

Cambodia re-introduced land ownership following the collapse of the Khmer Rouge in 1979 and the subsequent civil war. A 1989 law allows people who have occupied land for 5 years to claim ownership, but few have received deeds to the land while speculators are sitting on idle land (Economist 2007(a):68). Again, a transition to a stewardship economy could lead to more efficient land use and more equitable distribution of wealth.

Cuba

As Cuba makes its transition from communism to a market economy the key question is whether it will retain the rent of the land as revenue to be used for the common good, or whether it will gift its land and natural resources into private ownership.

The legacy of colonialism

Zimbabwe

After the second world war large tracts of what is now Zimbabwe were allocated by the colonial government to white settlers. Land reform was the main issue at the 1979 constitutional talks that led to independence, and Robert Mugabe came to power in 1980 with the promise to return land to black people. He was able to block the land tax proposals of his rival Joshua Nkomo, and the British government agreed to contribute £30 million to acquire 7.5 million acres on which 62,000 families were resettled (Economist 97: 81) In 1992 Mugabe changed the constitution to allow compulsory purchase of any land, and a programme of land reform since then has served to punish his critics and reward his friends and family while raising little revenue.

Bolivia

Many landowners in Bolivia owe their ownership rights to the land seizures and gifts of previous military governments. In spite of the success of Bolivia's first programme of land reform in 1953, 90 per cent of Bolivia's productive land is owned by 50,000 families (population of Bolivia 9.3 million) (Economist 2006:58) . In 1996 the registration of land title and a form of land tax were introduced, with land reverting to the state if the tax is not paid. In 2006 the government began to distribute titles to plots of government-owned land and promised also to redistribute private land that had been illegally acquired. Since then, a programme of land reform has led to violence.

Where there is a need to regularise private property in land and ensure that landholding is more widely distributed in the population, stewardship could provide a straightforward way of doing so.

Preparing for transitions in crisis

There are some parts of the world where it can be anticipated that crises of land ownership and land reform may arise rapidly. Apart from the question of Zimbabwe, there must be a possibility that a crisis will arise in any country in which land ownership is vested in the state rather than in individuals.

It would seem wise for the United Nations to be proactive and take steps to explore how to set about land reform where this is urgently needed, without waiting for violence to erupt. The key preparatory step is to make as much progress as possible with a survey that shows the land, its boundaries and improvements on it. Satellite imagery is now very detailed, allowing improvements to be documented. Informed guesswork would allow boundaries to be established that were good-enough to be used as a straw survey. This approach would need to be tested in advance in a country that wanted to establish an ownership database and was able to test such a survey against local intelligence.

Chapter 14 The environment in transition

This chapter explores how to make a transition from ownership to stewardship of the environment. This requires a move from gifting (grandfathering) permits either to taxation or to auctioning permits, an approach that already attracts wide support in many high-consumption economies. The section also describes how to distribute the revenue from renewable resources as an Environmental Dividend.

Property rights

The challenges of handling environmental property rights during transition are similar to, but different from, those relating to land ownership. In ownership economies many aspects of the environment are, or have recently been, the property of the state. States have managed some aspects of the environment directly as collective property, such as surface water resources; others, such as the atmosphere and the oceans, as open access regimes or common property. In yet others they have created private property rights either by giving them away to private owners, like fishing quotas; or by leasing them, as in the European Emissions Trading Scheme.

Transition from grandfathering to auctions

Where the environment is subject to private property rights, for example in the European Emissions Trading Scheme (Chapter 10), permits have been 'grandfathered' to firms who have been polluting or extracting. This has effectively legitimised their past behaviour and legalised their squatters rights. It has not compromised the efficiency of the tradable permits as a way of limiting emissions, but it cannot be described as fair as it represents a gift from governments to existing polluters.

The first step towards transition would be to set up national and international Environment Stewardship Trusts for each aspect of the environment. These trusts could manage the environment in a number of ways, including issuing permits to use each aspect of the environment.

For collective property the government would become the steward. Bodies need to be established, if none already exist, to act as stewards of common property.

If we were to introduce stewardship of the environment outright, without a transition mechanism, we would be confiscating existing private property rights, and this would cause economic disruption as well as perhaps not being entirely fair. On the other hand, the present owners' claim to these rights is far more insubstantial than the claims of existing landowners.

Stewardship Economy: private property without private ownership has proposed that, as far as land is concerned, existing property rights should be respected. The transition proposed for land ownership protects these rights indefinitely, but property rights to the environment only need to be protected for as long as is needed to enable their proprietors to adjust.

One possible transition from grandfathering to permit auctions would involve a ten year switch where:

In year 1, 100 per cent of the available permits are allocated to existing emitters and extractors in proportion to their use of the sink or resource in year zero.

In year 2, 90 per cent of the available permits are allocated in this proportion and 10 per cent are allocated by auction.

Each year a further 10 per cent of the permits are allocated by auction, so that after 10 years all the permits are allocated in this way.

This provides existing emitters and extractors a 10 year period in which to adapt to the new cost structures.

How to use the revenue from environmental charges

Ownership economy

In an ownership economy the revenue from environmental charges and taxes may be used in several possible ways:

- To reduce the level of other taxes – replacing taxes on 'goods' (e.g., work, adding value) with taxes on 'bads' (e.g., environmental damage, holding land out of use).

- For environmental purposes – to fund environmental protection measures, regulatory bodies or subsidies, for example.

- For the benefit of poorer people, as environmental charges and taxes tend to be regressive.

You might expect that a pound-for-pound reduction in other taxes would counter political resistance, but environmental charges are likely to be seen as a stealth tax because the electorate is suspicious and the government's tax revenues are complex and opaque.

Stewardship economy

In a stewardship economy, when there is a need to fund environmental measures the revenue comes from the government revenue (and so from stewardship fees for land) not from environmental charges.

Renewable resources

The whole of the revenue from the sale of permits for renewable resources is distributed to everyone on an equal per capita basis as an Environmental Dividend. As a result, those who use more than their equal share compensate those who use less than their equal share. This ensures that the poor are not disadvantaged and allays fears of stealth taxes in a fair and transparent way.

As mentioned earlier, there is likely to be an early stage of transition during which the Universal Income is subject to income tax. During this stage it would be important for everyone to receive their full equal share of the revenue for the use of renewable resources, as this ensures that the principle remains clear that high users of the environment compensate low users. This requires that the Environmental Dividend be paid to every individual without deduction of income tax and is one of the reasons for keeping the Environmental Dividend separate from the Universal Income.

Non-renewable resources

Revenue from non-renewable resources should ideally be invested in physical or human capital for the benefit of future generations, to meet the requirements of sustainability. If the state were to decide to distribute the revenue, this should be included as part of the Environmental.

Chapter 15 Parallel streams of transition

This chapter proposes one possible transition to a stewardship economy. It consists of three parallel strands, each with their own time-course. Proposals for the first strand, the **environment**, could be introduced immediately (Chapter 14).

The second strand, for **non-domestic properties,** would be possible to introduce in a fairly short time scale, as most businesses that make efficient use of land would feel an immediate direct benefit and there would be no opposition from homeowners. It would start with a Stage 1 reform in which the National Non-Domestic (Business) Rates are replaced by a Land Value Tax in a revenue-neutral fashion. In Stage 2 a Land Value Tax set at 100 per cent of any subsequent increase in the market rent of the land would be collected, with the revenue used to reduce other taxes on business.

The third strand, for **properties currently used for housing,** would begin with a reform of the Council Tax so that it is levied in proportion to the value of the property. This would be followed by a Stage 1 revenue-neutral replacement of Council Tax by a Land Value Tax. In Stage 2 a Land Value Tax set at 100 per cent of any subsequent increase in the market rent of the land would be collected, with the revenue used to reduce other taxes.

The necessary next step would be to model the proposed change to ensure that the detailed consequences are explored as thoroughly as possible. This modelling would need to be compared with the results of modelling the impact of other sets of proposals.

During transition it would be simplest and most transparent if the revenue from stewardship fees for the use of three aspects of the natural world – the environment, land used for domestic purposes and land used for non-domestic purposes – were treated separately. The whole of transition to stewardship could then be planned as three separate streams of work that could take place in parallel but without having to march in lock-step with each other. And all three groups of contributors – users of the environment, owners of domestic land and owners of non-domestic land – could clearly see that they were personally benefiting either from a reduction in the burden of their conventional taxes or from an income.

Non-domestic (business) land

The Mirrlees review, charged with proposing how the UK could move towards an optimal tax system, recommended the replacement of Non-Domestic (Business) Rates by a Land Value Tax (James Mirrlees et al 2011: 240). The Coalition for Economic Justice (2018) has outlined a proposal for a five year transitional reform of business rates. A detailed proposal for a feasibility study of replacement of National Non-Domestic (Business) Rates by a Land Value Tax is set out elsewhere (Julian Pratt 2015).

There are serious deficiencies in the National Non-Domestic (Business) Rates, particularly the infrequent valuations; the many reliefs and exemptions; valuation based on current use instead of the highest and best use that the land can be put to under the planning regulations; and incidence that generally falls on the occupier not the owner. However, the system of National Non-Domestic (Business) Rates has several good features that make it relatively straightforward to replace with a Land Value Tax. It is levied in proportion to market value (even if this is the market value of the whole property not just the land). And across the country as a whole, it levies about the right amount of revenue from business land.

Stage 1 transition– revenue-neutral replacement by LVT

It would not be difficult to implement a revenue-neutral replacement of National Non-Domestic (Business) Rates by a Land Value Tax. Owners of business land who have invested in appropriate improvements, and which can therefore be used efficiently, would be subject to lower levels of Land Value Taxation than the National Non-Domestic (Business) Rates they currently pay. Businesses that use land inefficiently by leaving it undeveloped would pay higher levels of Land Value Tax than the Non-Domestic (Business) Rates they currently pay. Land being used efficiently would rise in value, and land being used inefficiently would fall in value.

Stage 2 transition – replace other taxes on business

Once Stage 1 is complete, as land values rise over time and as more revenue from the Land Value Tax becomes available, other taxes that fall on and impede business would be candidates for reduction and removal. The way to get the greatest benefit from this is to remove one tax at a time rather than reduce taxes proportionately across the board, because the complete removal of a tax removes the costs of administration and collection, and this provides financial and efficiency savings.

Employers' National Insurance contributions are an obvious choice for removal as they push up the gross rates of pay that employers need to offer, create unnecessary bureaucracy for employers, distort employment patterns, act as a tax on jobs and fall most heavily on the lowest-paid. VAT should be next as it pushes up prices (reducing demand and economic activity), generates unnecessary bureaucracy by requiring businesses to act as unpaid tax-gatherers, distorts and diminishes the activity of businesses trying to keep below the VAT threshold, provides ample opportunities for fraud and falls most heavily on the poorest. Eventually there would be the opportunity to reduce and remove Corporation Tax.

Impact on stakeholders

The owners of commercial and industrial properties that make efficient use of their land within the limits set by the planning system would be net beneficiaries by paying Land Value Tax compared with National Non-Domestic (Business) Rates. Those that make inefficient use of their land would be net losers.

The overall result would be that stewardship fees for businesses would reward efficient land use and stimulate business development on marginal sites.

Where a business is not an owner-occupier of the property, but rather a landlord or tenant, costs and benefits of tax replacement fall asymmetrically on the landlord and tenant. The landlord bears the direct cost of the stewardship fees while most of the tax reductions benefit the tenant. Provided that the terms of the tenancy allow, rents will rise so that these compensatory benefits are passed on to the landlord. What the tenant gains from the tax shift will be lost in higher rents.

Agricultural land has been exempt from business rates since 1929. This exemption, intended to improve the profitability of farming, has failed to have the desired effect for entirely predictable reasons. It has brought no benefits to tenant farmers, who together farm more than a third of the agricultural area of England and Wales, or to farming contractors. Agricultural tenants are spared from paying business rates, but this releases them to offer higher rents (an insight known as the equation theory). The market rent is determined by the profitability of farming the land. Agricultural tenants derive no financial benefit, and farming is no more profitable than it was without the exemption. The exemption has enriched the owners of agricultural land and made farmland an attractive investment opportunity, indeed a speculative investment.

While exemption has benefited those who have inherited farms or who have paid off their mortgage, it has caused financial problems for anyone wanting to enter farming and buy land with a mortgage. Mortgage payments are inflated in line with the market value of the land, which is higher than expected from the market rent that a tenant is able and willing to pay. The yield (from farming income) on a potential landowner's investment is low – too low in general to pay the interest on the mortgage. So, until the mortgage is paid off, the owner-occupier can only manage financially if they have an additional source of income. This discourages new entrants to farming while farmland is bought by investors with no real interest in the practice of farming. A more distant consequence is that owners of commercial and industrial land, who do pay business rates, are burdened by cross-subsidising agricultural landowners.

Land Value Tax falls on the owners of land, and they would want to pass this cost on to their tenants by increasing their rent. They could only do so if the rent they were charging before Land Value Tax was below the market rent.

Any reform of the National Non-Domestic (Business) Rates that removes the reliefs and exemptions that it incorporates would reduce the market value of the land in question. There may be a case for applying an exemption for agricultural land during the first 5 years of a Land Value Tax, and for reviewing the situation then (Julian Pratt 2014: 11). This must not, however, delay the introduction of Stage 2.

Domestic land

In the UK the housing market fails to provide decent homes that everyone can afford. There are several areas in which reform is needed, including the provision of more homes at subsidised rents (social housing); improved terms, conditions and quality standards for private rental properties; planning processes that are more democratic and better-resourced than at present; and some increase in housing supply. Reforming Council Tax and replacing it with a Land Value Tax would have a major impact. The implementation of this stream of transition would complete the transition to a stewardship economy.

Introducing a Land Value Tax is a more complex challenge for domestic than for non-domestic land. One reason is that the Council Tax is, unlike the National Non-Domestic (Business) Rates, highly regressive and in no way proportional to the market value of a property (Chapter 2). Another reason is that since the abolition of Schedule A income tax on the imputed rent of an owner-occupied home in 1960s people have planned their financial future on the assumption that their home would be subject to only modest levels of taxation.

In addition, any reform of taxation of domestic land needs to move forward in parallel with a reform of the benefit system if it is to improve the financial position of the poorest. For all these reasons the proposal described here for domestic land starts with a reform of Council Tax, followed by two stages as for non-domestic land.

Revenue-neutral reform of Council Tax

Council Tax proportional to 1991 valuations

A revenue-neutral reform of the Council Tax, such that everyone in the country is paying the same proportion of the market value of their property (even based on 1991 valuations), would have a dramatic effect on many people's Council Tax bills. Within a billing authority those in lower-value properties would pay less and those in higher-value properties more. Across the country those in billing authorities with lower property values would pay less, those with higher property values would pay more.

Liability transferred to owner

This reform of the Council Tax would be the time to transfer the liability to pay the tax from occupier to owner. This makes no difference to owner-occupiers, but it does to tenants and landlords. Removing the liability for Council Tax from the tenant leads to an immediate increase in their disposable income. This would enable their landlord to increase their rent by the same amount, so the financial positions of the landlord and tenant would be unchanged, with the tenant paying a higher rent and the landlord paying the whole of this increased rent as Council Tax. This would probably require either a blanket legal change to all tenancy agreements or phasing in as tenancy agreements came up for review.

The intention in 1993 was that voters, that is to say residents not owners, should be the ones to pay the tax in the expectation that they would vote for councils that kept tax bills as low as possible. The amount of tax collected by a local authority in a fully developed stewardship economy depends on property values not the behaviour of the authority, so other ways need to be found to make authorities responsive to the wishes of voters. It is more appropriate for the owners of land, who are the ultimate beneficiaries of that land, to pay the tax.

Removal of discounts and exemptions

This transfer of liability would also be the best moment to remove the discounts and exemptions for particular occupants of domestic properties, who would face additional expenditure. There are reasons why society has decided to support these groups that generally remain cogent with the reform of Council Tax, and each group will need to be supported in the future in a different way (Chapter 2).

Impact of Council Tax reform

Turning what is more or less a disguised Poll Tax into a property tax that is even approximately proportional to property values would have a dramatic impact on many people's finances. A revenue-neutral reform would reduce the tax paid by lower-value homes (Bands A to C make up 65% of all homes).

High value homes, wherever they are in the country, would start to pay more, and in some cases much more, than they are now. This would be enough to reduce their market value, which would generate some resistance but to counteract opposition the reform could be promoted on the grounds that it would make Council Tax fairer. The reduction in Council Tax paid by owners of lower-value homes would pose a problem for councils in areas that are already suffering from deprivation. This would require transfer of revenue from prosperous to deprived areas.

Stage 1 transition – replace Council Tax with Land Value Tax

One advantage of starting transition with the replacement of Council Tax by a Land Value Tax is that the relatively large impact of making Council Tax fairer would help to reduce political opposition to a Land Value Tax. The impact of the Council Tax reform will have been significant, and for most people this will be amplified or moderated by the revaluation that follows. Changes can be seen as a necessary updating of Council Tax to remove its design flaws and take account of current property values. It also allows the revaluation to be carried out after the market has taken account of the Council Tax reform.

Revaluation of properties for Stage 1

Several factors will have changed the value of each property since 1991. The market value and market rent of all properties have increased. If each property had increased by the same proportion, there would be no need for a revaluation, as Stage 1 is designed to be revenue-neutral. But property values in some areas have risen a lot while property values in other areas have risen only a little. This means that a revenue-neutral switch to a property tax based on up to date values (even if this was based on the value of the whole property and the same banding as at present) would result in an increase in tax for properties in areas where market values have risen most and a reduction in in areas where they have risen least.

The Council Tax reform described above will itself affect the value of many properties. Broadly speaking, lower Council Tax on low-value homes will lead to an increase in their market value while higher Council Tax on high-value homes will lead to a decrease in their market value, though the removal of discounts and exemptions will complicate change.

In Stage 1 Council Tax is replaced by a Land Value Tax. Instead of a tax proportional to *the market value of the whole property*, it would become proportional to *the market rent of the land but not the building*. This means that a revaluation is needed before moving on to Stage 1 to identify the market rent of the land, excluding the value of the buildings and other improvements. In practice this means that the revaluation needs to establish the market rent of the land and the Depreciated Replacement Cost of the improvements (buildings). The principles of this valuation are discussed elsewhere (Chapter 7). The cost of the revaluation could be added in to the total Land Value Tax to be collected so that the revenue-neutrality was preserved even with this additional expenditure.

Impact of Stage 1

A Land Value Tax levied on the market rent of the land will have some impact on the tax to be paid on many properties. The change from a tax on the whole property to one based on the valuation of land alone (on the highest and best use) will benefit homes in good repair that are making good use of the land on which they are situated (within the limits imposed by the planning system); they will pay less as they will no longer be paying tax on the value of their buildings. Homes in poor repair, particularly those that are derelict (so previously subject to low levels of tax), and those making poor use of the available land would pay more under the new system. As a result, the market rent, and so the tax, for individual homes would rise or fall accordingly, but the magnitude of the change would be relatively small. This is because, unlike non-domestic land, housing land is already in its highest and best use (housing) and most homes are in reasonable repair.

The change from market value to market rent will make little difference to the tax paid, as yields do not vary a great deal between different types of property and around the country..

In spite of the similarity between the Stage 1 proposals for domestic and non-domestic land, there is a critical difference. For non-domestic land the resulting Land Value Tax will be not far from equal to the market rent of the land. For domestic land, because Council Tax currently collects only a small proportion of the market rent of most housing land, the resulting 'Stage 1 Land Value Tax' will probably only amount to about 10% of the total stewardship fees that would be collected in an ideal world.

For many advocates of Land Value Taxation this may seem completely inadequate as it leaves most of the market rent and market value in the hands of the owner. The reason for this proposal is to honour the expectations and financial viability of existing owners by not confiscating the value of their property. But see Stage 2.

Stage 2 transition– taxing any increase in market rent of land

Throughout Stage 2 owners of domestic property continue to pay their 'Stage 1 Land Value Tax'. At the beginning of Stage 2 the New Land Market is introduced as described under 'practical proposal for valuation' (Chapter 11). The Transitional Value is set equal to the market value of the whole property, and the 'Stage 2 Land Value Tax' is set at zero.

Any increase in market rent from the start of Stage 2 is subject to a tax of 100%. This means that the market value of land is capped at the level it had at the end of Stage 1, no further increases are to be anticipated and land ceases to be an investment with a speculative element.

The revenue from Stage 2 Land Value Tax is then available to reform the tax system, removing existing taxes with their deadweight loss.

Impact of Stage 2

Provided that people believe the reform is not going to be repealed, Stage 2 has an enormous impact even before a penny is paid in Stage 2 Land Value Tax. Unlike the introduction of a full-blooded Land Value Tax as advocated by Henry George, there would be no reduction in the value of people's homes and so no threat to the banking system. But at a stroke our present expectations that house prices will go on rising would be removed.

Anyone buying a house would, just like the buyer of a car, expect to be able to sell it for a roughly similar sum of money minus any depreciation of the buildings. The great financial advantage that owner-occupiers have over renters would be immediately abolished. We could look forward to a future in which, for those who want to buy, homes would become less expensive and mortgages smaller.

Taxation that is both local and national

Council Tax is a local tax. It provides about 25 per cent of the total revenue required by a council, with the rest provided by central government in the form of the Revenue Support Grant and redistribution of part of the National Non-Domestic (Business) Rates.

Stage 2 Land Value Tax should be used to provide revenue both for local and national government. One way to do this would be to allocate to each local council the same proportion of the total national Stage 2 Land Value Tax, weighted according to population and perhaps according to some measure of deprivation. This proportion should be enough to meet the budgetary needs of the council that has the greatest level of expenditure, with the rest going to central government.

In this way both local and national government would ultimately receive in revenue that is more than they need for their expenditure and would distribute the remainder as a Universal Income (which would thus have a local and a national component). Political parties could then go to the polls at both local and national elections proposing a quite different mix of service provision and Universal Income.

Using the revenue from Stage 2 Land Value Tax

An obvious candidate for reduction and removal would be Stamp Duty Land Tax on domestic properties as this reduces land values and causes inefficiencies in the property market. Another would be employees' National Insurance contributions which fall disproportionately on low-paid workers, discourage employment and are a significant organisational burden on employers (employers' National Insurance contributions should already have been removed as part of the reform of National Non-Domestic (Business) Rates). They are a deterrent to flexible and part-time working as they are complicated and penalise people who have a combination of employment and self-employment or multiple employers. Reductions in National Insurance contributions are likely to translate into higher take-home pay.

Income tax could then be phased out if there was the political will to do so. The simplest approach would probably be to increase the personal allowance so that more and more people are removed from the tax net. Simply increasing the allowance delivers the greatest absolute gains to the highest earners as it reduces the amount of income that is subject to the higher rate of tax, so it would be important to ensure that it could only be deducted from income liable to the basic tax rate. Capital Gains Tax, too, could be reduced once the rate of income tax had fallen to the level at which Capital Gains Tax is levied. Finally, revenue from residential properties could be used to replace Inheritance Tax if that was the political choice.

Using the revenue from Stage 2 Land Value Tax is, however, very little help to the poorest members of society who pay no income tax or national insurance contributions. They benefit only when some of the revenue is used to reduce the level of VAT. For this reason, some of the revenue should be used to reform the benefit system and introduce a Universal (Basic) Income (Chapter 12).

Impact on stakeholders

The immediate effect of transferring liability for paying the tax from tenant to landlord is that tenants would benefit and landlords would pay the Land Value Tax. The temporary increase in tenants' disposable income would allow landlords to charge a higher rent for the property, so market rents of these rental properties would rise. Landlords would, in general, recoup in rents what they lose in stewardship fees when the liability to pay the tax is transferred to them. Tenants, such as students, who are exempt from Council Tax, would be unable to afford higher rents and this would limit the increase in rents that landlords could charge. These landlords would either absorb the cost, rent to tenants who had previously paid Council Tax and could afford to pay more, or sell their properties.

In Stage 2 where the revenue is used to reduce or remove existing taxes, landlords of properties that are rising rapidly in value will find themselves paying more in stewardship fees than they gain from reductions in other taxes, while landlords of properties that are falling in value, or rising only slowly, are likely overall to be beneficiaries.

Owner-occupiers as a whole would find that falling Council Tax bills broadly offset their Land Value Tax. But Council Tax currently falls disproportionately on people occupying less valuable properties, so people living in these properties would benefit more from transition to stewardship. People in high value properties would contribute more as the result of transition, particularly those currently paying little tax on earned income like the unemployed and many pensioners. Owners of empty and second homes, who may not currently pay the full Council Tax, would also contribute more.

During the tax-replacement cycle, as orthodox taxes are replaced by Land Value Tax, owner-occupiers of modest properties, particularly those who pay a lot of income tax, benefit from falling taxes. Owner-occupiers with more valuable properties (per capita) will benefit only if they initially pay significant amounts of income tax and will be net contributors if they initially pay little tax. Overall, owners of properties on less desirable land would gain and owners of properties on more desirable land would lose.

Here are some examples of how individuals might be affected during transition to a stewardship economy:

A is a single person, in work and receiving no benefits. She earns £40,000 per year and bought her home recently for £120,000 (UK average in 2002), paying £6,000 per year in mortgage interest. The market rent of her land is rising by £500 per year (equivalent in an ownership economy to a rise in capital value of 5 per cent).

From the onset of transition, she faces a growing expenditure on the stewardship fees for her home of £500 per year, but she also benefits from a slowly growing Universal Income and from tax cuts that broadly compensate her. The big change is that her home is no longer an investment but a slowly depreciating asset.

B & C are a professional couple with a child of 4 years old. They bought their home recently for £480,000, paying £24,000 a year in mortgage interest. They receive child benefit but no other benefits. The market rent of their land is rising by £2000 per year (equivalent in an ownership economy to a rise in capital value of 5 per cent).

As land values rise they begin to pay a stewardship fee that rises by £2000 per year. They benefit from cuts in VAT and so on, and all three receive a Universal Income, though this is taxed as income. Their benefit package is reduced by 33p for every £ of Universal Income they receive. So, when the total family income from Universal Income is three times their original benefit package (1.8 times more once income tax has been paid at 40 per cent), they stop drawing child benefit. This occurs when the individual Universal Income is equal to the previous level of child benefit – if they had 2 children it would occur when the individual Universal Income is ¾ of the original level of child benefit.

D is a single person who earns £12,000 per year, gets no benefits and pays £5,000 per year in rent.

As the market rent of the land on which her home is located rises by £400 per year from the onset of transition, her rent rises accordingly. The difference from an ownership economy is that tax cuts and the Universal Income broadly compensate her for the increased rent.

If she was living in a more expensive home – or, rather, a home that increased in market rent by more than £400, she would do worse. If in a less expensive home, she would benefit even more.

The increased rent enables the landlord to pay the stewardship fee. But the landlord makes no additional profit as rents go up, and her asset is gradually depreciating

E & F are a couple with two children. They earn £18,000 a year from employment and receive child benefit and working families tax credit. They pay £7,000 per year in rent.

As the market rent of the land on which their home is located rises by £500 per year from the onset of transition, their rent rises accordingly. The difference from an ownership economy is that tax cuts and the Universal Incomes (4* £X) broadly compensate them for the increase in rent. Their benefit package of £Y (two child benefits and the working families tax credits) is reduced by 33p for every £ of Universal Income they receive.

So, when the total family income from Universal Income is three times their original benefit package (2.4 times more once income tax has been paid at 20 per cent), they stop drawing child benefit.

If they were living in a more expensive home – or, rather, a home that increased in market rent by more than £500, they would do worse. If in a less expensive home, they would benefit more.

The increased rent they pay enables the landlord to pay the stewardship fee. But the landlord makes no additional profit as rents go up, and her asset is gradually depreciating.

G is a single parent with children of 8 and 10. She rents her home. She receives child benefit, working families tax credit, housing benefit etc.

As the market rent of the land on which her home is located rises by £500 per year from the onset of transition, her rent rises accordingly. The difference from an ownership economy is that tax cuts and the Universal Incomes (4* £X) broadly compensate for the increase in rent. Her benefit package of £Y (two child benefits and the working families tax credits) is reduced by 33p for every £ of Universal Income she receives. So, when the total family income from Universal Income is three times their original benefit package (2.4 times more once income tax has been paid at 20 per cent), she stops drawing child benefit.

As in previous examples, if G was living in a more expensive home – or, rather, a home that increased in market rent by more than £500, she would do worse. If in a less expensive home, she would benefit more. The increased rent they pay enables the landlord to pay the stewardship fee. But the landlord makes no additional profit as rents go up, and her asset is gradually depreciating.

Impact on poverty

In the UK about 13 million people, 20 per cent of the population, were living in poverty in 2008. The UK uses the OECD

(Organisation for Economic Cooperation and Development) definition of poverty – an income of less than 60 per cent of the median income for households of the same kind. The 60 per cent levels are (Polly Toynbee and David Walker 2008:76):

	2006/7 60 % median income	2008 60 % of median income	Universal Income
Single adult	£112 per week		£64.30 pw
2-adult, no children	£193 pw	£217 pw	£128.60 pw
2 adult, 1 child			£202.01 pw
Single adult, 2 children	£189 pw	£260 pw	£211.12 pw
Couple, 2 children	£270 pw	£332 pw	£275.42 pw

These figures are measured after income tax, Council Tax and housing costs have been deducted, where housing costs include rents, mortgage interest (but not the repayment of principal), buildings insurance and water charges. http://www.poverty.org.uk/

A Universal Income alone would provide families with two children with enough income to lift them above current poverty levels. Most of the 20 per cent of UK families below the poverty line are amongst the 27 per cent who rent their home. These families would face no additional expense from the introduction of stewardship fees. Families with one child or none are not projected to obtain enough income from the Universal Income to lift them above the current poverty line, and they would need additional support to do so.

Summary

This final chapter has described three parallel strands for the introduction of Land Value Taxation.

- New charges, fees, fees or taxes for the use of the environment are introduced with the whole of the revenue distributed as an equal per capita Environmental Dividend.

- Non-domestic land fees, in Stage 1, the replacement of National Non-Domestic (Business) Rates with Land Value Tax in a revenue-neutral way. In Stage 2 the revenue from subsequent increases in the market rent of non-domestic land is used to reduce other taxes on business.

- Domestic land first sees a revenue-neutral transformation of Council Tax into a tax that is directly proportional to the market rent of the property (land + buildings). In Stage 1 this is replaced, again in a revenue-neutral way, by a Land Value Tax. In Stage 2 the revenue from subsequent increases in the market rent of domestic land is used to replace existing taxes and, where feasible, introduce a Universal Income.

These three strands could be implemented independently according to their own independent timetables, in parallel. The simplest transition, the one that applies to the environment, could be implemented more or less immediately. Transition for non-domestic land could take place in five to ten years, while transition for domestic land to a stewardship economy would take longer.

www.ingramcontent.com/pod-product-compliance
Lightning Source LLC
Chambersburg PA
CBHW051212170526
45166CB00005B/1856